RECIPES FOR TIRED TEACHERS
Well-Seasoned Activities for Language Learning

Contributed by teachers associated with
Pilgrims Language Courses
Canterbury, England

EDITED BY CHRIS SION

ALTA BOOK CENTER PUBLISHERS—SAN FRANCISCO
14 Adrian Court, Burlingame, California 94010 USA

The Author

Chris Sion has taught English as a Foreign Language and been involved in teacher training since 1973. He has worked in several countries and has held posts in private language schools, universities, and in industry. He has been associated with Pilgrims Language Courses for many years.

In addition to publishing numerous articles in teaching journals, he is the author of *Creating Conversation in Class* and *Talking Business in Class* (Delta), and *Talking to Yourself in English* (Training Etcetera).

Chris is married, has two children, and lives in the Netherlands, very near the German and Belgian borders.

Acquisitions Editor: Aaron Berman

Content and Production Editors:
Jamie Ann Cross and Raissa Nina Burns

Cover Design: Bruce Marion Design
Publisher's note regarding the cover design: In the United States, since the days of the one-room schoolhouse, an apple placed anonymously on the teacher's desk has represented a student's appreciation and admiration for his or her teacher.

Interior Design and Illustrations: Natesh Daniel

Original Copyright 1985 by Addison-Wesley Publishing Company, Inc.

 ALTA BOOK CENTER PUBLISHERS
14 Adrian Court
Burlingame, California 94010

Website: www.altaesl.com • Email: info@altaesl.com
Phone: 800 ALTA/ESL or 650 692 1285 (International)
Fax: 800 ALTA/FAX or 650 692 4654 (International)

ISBN 1-932383-00-X
Library of Congress Control Number: 2004101329

Dedicated to all those language students
throughout the world who are just sitting
there in class . . .

Introduction

Background

After nearly two decades in an edition published by Addison-Wesley, *Recipes for Tired Teachers* has been updated by Alta Book Center Publishers, giving the classic ideas it contains a fresh start in the 21st century. Teachers originally developed the activities at the summer sessions of Pilgrims Language Courses in Canterbury, England. The recipes grew from teaching experience gathered all over he world—from Chile to China, from Korea to California, from Western Europe, the Middle East, Japan, and Australia to Romania, Turkey, South Africa, and Brazil.

Scope

The ideas reflect the individuality and diverse professional backgrounds of the authors. In addition to being English teachers, the contributors' backgrounds include modern languages, politics, philosophy, journalism, and commerce. The collection includes role simulations, language games, and creativity exercises. There are group dynamics encounters, which will appeal especially to teachers interested in psychology, and job-related material for teachers working with business students or in industry. The pages include a wealth of tasks for conversation, plus activities for practicing and improving listening, reading, and writing skills. Some activities center on a linguistic function, others on a grammatical structure. A few have a lexical orientation and focus on vocabulary. There are icebreakers for getting new groups going and feedback activities for keeping in touch with the students' feelings and perceptions.

Adaptability

Recipes for Tired Teachers contains exercises for all learning levels. Most of them can be used with or adapted for any age group. Although originally conceived for Teaching English as a Foreign Language, the activities can be used to teach any language at all. They also have a place in general studies and literacy skills courses.

Being brief and self-contained, the recipes may be used in many ways. They are especially helpful to the teacher whose class is "bogged down" and who needs a change of pace or who wants to fill an empty half-hour with a lively lesson. But they may also be molded into a syllabus or used to introduce or consolidate a teaching point. By keeping an eye open, creative teachers will find countless opportunities in which the ideas will enliven their classes and stimulate the students.

Practical Information

The contributions have been divided into eight units on the basis of their major emphasis. Each recipe features information about the contributors, the approximate time needed, the level, the main language function(s) dealt with, and the materials required. It is assumed that the usual classroom fixtures will be available, including a board (be it a chalkboard or whiteboard) or its equivalent (flip chart, newsprint pad, overhead projector), and that students will have paper and pens. Accordingly, these are not listed under "Materials" at the top of the recipe. Nor are incidental items such as scissors and paste mentioned in every case. If preparation is required, this is stated under the "Before Class" heading, unless the only preparation necessary is familiarizing oneself with the content.

Style

The authors' diversity is also reflected in the way they express themselves. As the editor, my task has been not only to select and classify the recipes, but also to establish a thread of cohesion in the style and format without losing the personal spark of each of the contributors. The editorial changes have been made with a view to making the instructions clear, accessible, and relevant to the modern world. The goal has been to produce a user-friendly book for language teachers.

Approach

The creative impulse of the teacher in bringing the ideas to life is natural and should be encouraged. Just as a good cook does more than blindly follow a recipe, so does a good teacher add his or her own special flavoring to an activity. Feel free to condense or expand, to adjust the language up or down, to change a pair activity to a small group activity, and to make whatever modifications will be effective in your teaching situation. I sincerely hope that teachers who try these recipes will not simply rehash them, but will accept them as outlines and suggestions to be adapted to the needs and interests of their students and to their own personalities. My vision is of the process of teaching/learning truly becoming one of *re-creation*.

Acknowledgements

Sources for the contributions have been cited wherever possible, although the problem of establishing originality persists. Responses from the contributors have been along such lines as "It grew out of a party game/workshop/article/misunderstanding, and as far as I know has not been developed in TEFL or TESL . . . ." If a teacher comes across a teaching idea, modifies it, and then demonstrates it at a seminar, where a colleague likes it, adapts it, and describes it to a student, who passes it on (including a few changes) to a friend, who in turn personalizes it and writes it up, who is to get the credit? As Gertrude Moscowitz observes in *Caring and Sharing in the Foreign Language Classroom* (Newbury House, 1978), "Tracking down . . . activities to their original source can be as difficult as determining the creators of folklore or legends. The origin of some exercises is not traceable; they just seem to be handed down." Any lack of proper acknowledgment in this book is unintentional.

Thanks

I should like to thank Mario Rinvolucri and James Dixey of Pilgrims Language Courses in Canterbury, and Mike Lavery and Martin Worth of the 3M Company in Neuss, Germany, for their help and encouragement; and, of course, the contributors for their contributions. A special word of appreciation should also go to my late London agent, Dick Evans, for all his advice and assistance; to Tab Hamlin for his editorial improvements to the original edition; and to Aaron Berman and Jamie Cross of Alta Book Center Publishers for their enthusiasm for *Recipes for Tired Teachers* and for keeping the book alive. A further acknowledgment goes to Saxon Menné for suggesting the title.

The final credit goes to my personal "in-house" coach, consultant, and educational advisor, my wife, Kathleen, for always being there when I need her help.

Chris Sion

Table of Recipes

Unit 1–Group Dynamics

Unit 2–Creative Writing and Thinking

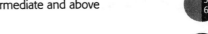

Unit 3–Reading and Writing

Unit 4–Listening

Unit 5–Role-Playing

Unit 6-Structures and Functions

Unit 7-Vocabulary (Lexis)

Index

Group Dynamics

1 You Are What You Will

Level
Intermediate and above

30–60

Language Functions
Imagining

Asking and answering questions

MATERIALS
None

BEFORE CLASS
Requires no preparation!

1 Tell the class that they are to imagine another life. In this new life they can take the form of an animal, a plant, or an object. The one form they cannot take is that of a human being. Give them a few minutes to think about what they would like to be.

2 Then ask the students, one at a time, to say what they are and to describe themselves. Encourage the other students to ask anything they like about the new personality, its function, background, feelings, and so on.

3 After the students have revealed and described their new identities, conduct a general feedback discussion. Help the students to analyze what they have learned about themselves and one another and about human aspirations in general. You may also want to elicit discussion of possible contrasts between the students' "new life" and "real life" identities in terms of such criteria as age, sex, nationality, or any others that may show up in the course of the lesson.

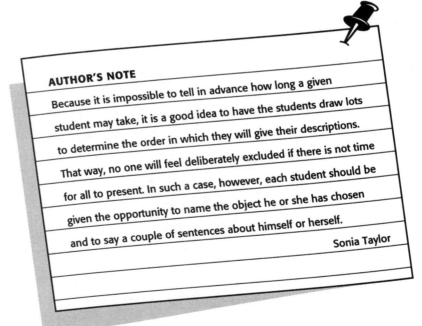

AUTHOR'S NOTE

Because it is impossible to tell in advance how long a given student may take, it is a good idea to have the students draw lots to determine the order in which they will give their descriptions. That way, no one will feel deliberately excluded if there is not time for all to present. In such a case, however, each student should be given the opportunity to name the object he or she has chosen and to say a couple of sentences about himself or herself.

Sonia Taylor

Neighbors

Level
Intermediate and above

50

Language Functions
Describing

Imagining

MATERIALS	BEFORE CLASS
None	Requires no preparation!

1 Tell students to take a piece of paper and draw a house on it. They are to work alone. When the houses are drawn, they are to fold the papers in two so that the houses cannot be seen. The papers are collected, placed in the center of the table, and shuffled. Each student then picks one and unfolds it.

2 Now ask the students, one at a time, to describe in detail the house on the paper each has chosen. Ask them to describe the occupants of the house, the furniture in the house, the colors used in the different rooms, the location of the house, and any other details they can think of.

3 Next, arrange all the drawings face up on the table. Ask each student to choose one that he or she likes and write his or her name on the back of it. There should be only one name on each drawing.

4 Then have the class, working together, arrange the houses in groups of three. (If the number of drawings is not divisible by three, one or two groups may have four houses.) Let the students develop their own criteria for grouping the houses. Provide no more guidance than "houses that you think go together well."

5 When the sets of houses are formed, ask those whose names appear on the drawings to sit together and create a three-minute skit that illustrates or depicts the relationship among the "neighbors" who live in the three (or four) houses.

6 Have the groups take turns to present their skits.

Author
John Morgan

3 Lying: An Icebreaker

Level
Low intermediate
and above

30–40

Language Functions
Disguising the truth

Exchanging and
comparing personal
information

MATERIALS	BEFORE CLASS
None	Requires no preparation!

1 Have the students form pairs. (If this activity is done at the beginning of the course as suggested, you may wish to assign the pairs yourself, since the students may not know one another and may feel bashful about pairing off.)

2 Tell the students they are to talk to their partners about themselves. One partner will talk while the other takes notes. Then they reverse roles. Tell them that they can reveal as much or as little as they like, but that *about three-quarters of what they say should be lies.*

3 Have the students repeat this process two or three times with different partners. Each time they meet a new partner, they give different information. However, the information should be about the same areas. In other words, they talk about the *same subjects* with each partner but tell *different lies* about these subjects to each partner.

4 Now have the students report back to the whole group about what they heard from each of their partners, using the notes they took in each interview as a guide. As each student reports, all those who met the same person listen carefully and then point out the discrepancies between the stories that person told. The fun comes in trying to decide what the truth really is, with everyone speculating about everyone else.

5 Each person finally tells the truth, leaving everybody knowing something about him or her.

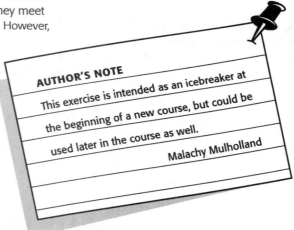

AUTHOR'S NOTE

This exercise is intended as an icebreaker at the beginning of a new course, but could be used later in the course as well.

Malachy Mulholland

Am I Lying? **4**

MATERIALS

Pictures
(see *Method Two* below)

BEFORE CLASS

Requires no preparation!

Level
Low intermediate
and above

20–30

Language Functions
Asking questions

Evaluating content

Telling or disguising
the truth

1

Method One

Tell a short anecdote which may either be true or be a complete fabrication. Have the group ask you questions about it. Give additional information as necessary to generate more questions. Then ask the students to decide whether you were telling the truth or making the whole thing up. Put it to a vote.

Method Two

A variation is to bring a picture (which the students cannot see) and describe it to the class. Again, the description may be true or it may be completely false. Let the group quiz you about the details. As with *Method One,* the students must decide whether you are telling the truth or lying.

2

To follow up, ask a student to tell a story or describe a picture in the same way. Again, the remainder of the class must decide whether the student is telling the truth or lying.

3

As an optional extra with either method, you may wish to ask students to explain why they voted as they did. This can be done individually, student by student, or by a panel of three or four students. Encourage the students to give contextual reasons for their verdicts rather than make comments such as "He or she always lies/exaggerates."

AUTHORS' NOTE

For *Method Two,* it is a good idea to use an "unlikely" picture—perhaps even an abstract or surrealistic one—the first time you do this exercise. This will create an atmosphere in which the improbable is on a par with one's more "normal" expectations.

Joan Hewitt

Chris Sion

5 Information Extraction

Level
Intermediate

20–30

Language Function
Asking questions

MATERIALS	BEFORE CLASS
None	Requires no preparation!

1 Divide the class into groups of three. One of the persons in each group is the questioner, another is the answerer, and the third is the umpire.

2 Tell the questioner to write on a slip of paper something he or she wants to know about the answerer, and give the slip to the umpire.

3 Now tell the questioner that his or her job is to extract the information on the slip from the answerer *without directly asking the question he or she has written down.* The umpire's job is to make sure the questioner follows this rule and does not ask the question directly or

change a question in midstream. To do this, the umpire can stop the questioner at any time. You may wish to give each questioner a time limit to expedite the exercise, or you may leave it to the group to impose, or not to impose, a time limit.

4 When the questioner has extracted the information, or the time limit has been passed, the members swap roles or start again.

Author
William Atkinson

Personality Test 6

MATERIALS	BEFORE CLASS
Grid (page 8)	Photocopy the grid. You may also want to copy Figure 1 on the board, but keep it covered until you are ready to use it (see Step 2).

Level
Intermediate and above

30–40

Language Functions
Interpreting visual stimuli

Discussing personal perception

1 Distribute copies of the grid. Tell the students that they are to make a drawing in each of the twelve squares. Eleven of the squares have small figures in them. These figures are to be incorporated into the drawings in the particular rectangles. Each drawing must be separate from the others: students may *not* combine two or more drawings to make one large drawing.

2 Once the drawings are complete, have the students write the following words on them in the corresponding squares (Figure 1). If you have made a large copy of Figure 1 as described (see *Before Class*), it can be uncovered at this time and students may copy the words from it.

You	Others	God
Death	Gift to Yourself	Love
Security	You and Your Surroundings	Your Surroundings
Aspirations	Balance	Spirit

Figure 1

3 Then give the class the following definitions or explanations of the words they have written on their drawings:

YOU: How you view yourself.

OTHERS: How you view other people.

GOD: Your view of religion.

DEATH: They way you regard death.

GIFT TO YOURSELF: Something you would like to give yourself.

LOVE: Your idea of love.

SECURITY: Your idea of security.

YOU AND YOUR SUR-ROUNDINGS: How you see yourself in relation to your surroundings.

YOUR SURROUNDINGS: How you regard your surroundings.

ASPIRATIONS: The way you see your aspirations, aims, and goals.

BALANCE: How you balance the forces in your life; your sense of (spiritual) balance.

SPIRIT: Your sense of spirit, energy, enthusiasm, liveliness.

4 Finally, divide the students into pairs to discuss their interpretations of their drawings and the ways in which these drawings could represent or correspond to the labels they wrote on them in Step 2.

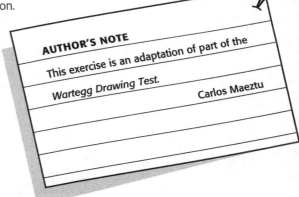

AUTHOR'S NOTE

This exercise is an adaptation of part of the Wartegg Drawing Test.

Carlos Maeztu

◁	♡	▯	⫽
᫛	▯	●	⫽
●	✕		⫽

The Last Time: An Encounter

MATERIALS	BEFORE CLASS	**Level**
None	Requires no preparation!	Intermediate

Level
Intermediate

45

Language Function
Exchanging and comparing personal information

1 Ask the students, one by one, to talk about a simple recent incident. They should use questions. For example:

The last time you paid a bill: Where were you? How much was the bill? What was it for? Do you prefer cash or checks?

The last time you used a computer: What did you use it for? Was it at home or at work? How many hours a day do you work on the computer on average? Do you enjoy using the computer? Can you cope if something goes wrong? In which room is your computer at home? How do you decide who can use the computer in your family?

Give enough time for the answerer to remember, but keep the pace brisk. Prompt with your own examples when necessary. Make it very clear that the "last time" element is just a lever to provoke discussion. If a student says he or she can't remember the last bill payment or phone call, or that it concerned something personal, ask him or her to talk about any recent example, or switch to another subject.

2 Collect a set of about twenty-five "last time" examples and write them on the board. Elicit as many as you can from the group, but be sure there is a good mix of everyday and personal items. A typical list might include:

- The last thing you bought
- The last joke you heard
- The last letter you wrote
- The last word you looked up
- The last class you attended
- The last present you gave

• The last time you:
   used a cell-phone
   surfed the Internet
   shook hands
   entertained
   were surprised
   played a game
   ate out
   ate alone
   kissed someone
   felt depressed
   gave money to charity
   were angry
   made someone angry
   made a mistake
   had a practical joke
      played on you

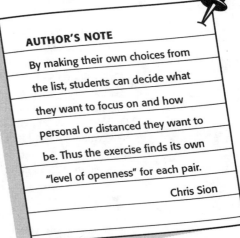

AUTHOR'S NOTE

By making their own choices from the list, students can decide what they want to focus on and how personal or distanced they want to be. Thus the exercise finds its own "level of openness" for each pair.

Chris Sion

• The last time you:
   overslept
   went to religious services
   went to a film or a concert
   went to the theater or the zoo
   stayed in a hotel
   really laughed
   made (or broke) a promise
   told a lie
   were lied to
   gave in (or didn't give in) to temptation
   played a practical joke

3 Divide the class into pairs and have each pair choose about twelve of the situations on the board to discuss. (If they wish, they may choose more and go into less detail on them, or fewer and spend more time on each; the decision is theirs.)

4 Let the pairs discuss the points they have chosen.

8 We'll Answer for You

Level
Intermediate

20–40

Language Function
Asking and answering
personal questions

MATERIALS	BEFORE CLASS
None	Requires no preparation!

1 Tell the group that you are ready to answer questions about yourself. Tell them they may ask fairly deep questions; they do not need to confine themselves to superficial questions, such as "What are your hobbies?" Suggest that each student write ten questions he or she would like to ask.

2 As students write their questions, circulate around the room, supplying words they are short of and helping with the formulation of questions as necessary. (Help students only with the most recent sentences they have written; if a student is composing question 7, a mistake in question 1 may be several light years behind him or her in emotional time.)

3 When everyone has written eight to ten questions, pick out those students with whom you feel the greatest empathy (those you believe will best be able to read and interpret you). Ask these students to sit in a crescent behind you, facing the rest of the group. Collect the questions from the group in the crescent and give them to the remainder of the class.

4 Now sit down facing the people with the questions and invite them to fire both their own questions and those of the people in the crescent at you. Tell them that the people in the crescent *are going to answer for you* and that you will remain silent.

Deny the questioners eye contact, but silently react to the answers given by your "doubles" or "alter egos" behind you. It is important that the doubles should be able to "read your back"—to understand from subtle body-language cues how you react to the answers they give.

The degree to which you concentrate on what is going on will strongly influence the power of the exercise.

5 Have a "debriefing" discussion with the group. How confident did the "doubles" feel in the answers they gave for you? Did their confidence increase or decrease as the questioning continued? How did the remainder of the group feel about the accuracy of the doubles' answers?

6 If there is time, and students are interested, you may want to repeat the exercise with another participant in the "hot seat."

AUTHOR'S NOTE

This exercise is best used early in a course, before students have very much factual knowledge about one another. But the mood of the group must be right for it; do not use the exercise with a group that is not ready for it.

The exercise is a variation of one proposed by John Morgan, in which members of a group ask a picture questions, while others in the group double for the picture. We learned the concept of "doubling" from Moreno's work in psychodrama. For my introduction to the application of psychodrama to language teaching, I have to thank Bernard Dufeu of Mainz University.

Mario Rinvolucri

Discussion Tactic

MATERIALS	**BEFORE CLASS**
Cartoon figures (page 12)	Photocopy the cartoon figures. You will need one copy for each class member plus at least one extra copy. Cut the extra copy into pieces so that there will be one character for each student. Leave one or two students out. For these students, prepare blank slips of the same sized paper with the instructions, "Say what you really think."

Level
Intermediate and above

45

Language Functions
Discussing

Justifying

Expressing opinions and feelings

1 Distribute the cut-out slips to the students. Either give a deliberately selected apposite (or inapposite) cartoon to each student, or put all the slips into a hat or bag and let each student take one. (This random assignment of characters to students can relax some of the tensions the group may feel about expressing negative feelings.)

2 Tell the class that they have ten to fifteen minutes for a discussion to be chaired by one of them. The discussion should concern the material they have been given, but no one should directly reveal the content of his or her piece of paper. Instead, students are to respond in character, but without actually quoting the words on their paper. During the discussion, circulate among the students, correcting and helping with vocabulary as necessary.

3 Stop the discussion after about fifteen minutes and pass out copies of the entire page of cartoon figures. Ask the class to identify which students were taking the parts of which cartoon characters and who was telling the truth—saying what he or she really thought. Ask students to justify their answers.

4 At this point students frequently begin to clarify their attitudes. Select as a new chairperson one of the students who had drawn a slip marked "Say what you really think," and begin a fresh discussion in which people express their real feelings.

AUTHOR'S NOTE

Students will participate more honestly and vigorously in the genuine discussion (Step 4) than they would without the use of Steps 1, 2, and 3. "Discussion Tactic" is a good exercise to get a new or inhibited group to open up or to broach a "danger topic" such as how students really feel about the course. The cartoon characters and the sentences attributed to them can be adapted to elicit opinions on other sensitive topics.

Joan Hewitt

Mr. A: Why should I have to listen to other foreign students' mistakes? The teacher should talk most of the time.

Ms. B: I just want to enjoy myself—fun and games for everyone!

Ms. C: I hate serious discussions—politics for example. When people disagree there is a very unpleasant atmosphere in the class. Learning should be fun.

Ms. D: I like people—knowing another language means I can meet *more* people. Making mistakes isn't really important if I can communicate.

Mr. E: Most teachers talk too much and dominate the lesson.

Ms. F: Actually I can learn more from a good textbook than from discussion groups and oral practice.

Mr. G: As an intellectual, I find language useful only to be polite or make social conversation in English.

Mr. H: Don't ask me—the teacher knows best.

Ms. I: Grammar is necessary before everything else. Once you know it, *then* you can begin speaking.

Is it Really Important?

MATERIALS	BEFORE CLASS
None	Requires no preparation!

Level
Low intermediate
and above

Language Functions
Comparing ideas

Justifying decisions

1 Divide the class into groups of four to six students.

2 Ask the students, working as individuals, to write down five words that they associate with their group. These should be words that might have relevance for any of the group's members.

3 Have each group produce a combined list of all the words chosen by the group's members. Then ask them to cull the list by crossing out or discarding 20% of the words. Each group member should then make a personal copy of the culled list for use in Step 4.

4 Working again as individuals, each student draws two columns next to the list of words. In the first column, next to each word, the student writes a number expressing the significance of the word to him/herself. Numbers run from 0 to 10, with 0 indicating no importance and 10 indicating great importance. In the second column, the student rates each word for someone else in the group, using the same numbering system. For example, if "television" were the word, a student might rate it as a 3 for him/herself, since he or she prefers reading, but might rate it as an 8 for a group member he or she knows is saving up for a new TV.

5 Compare and discuss the results. Were there words that were consistently chosen by all groups? Were there wide variations in the ratings? Can students explain why they rated some words high and others low? Can they justify their ratings of the supposed preferences of others?

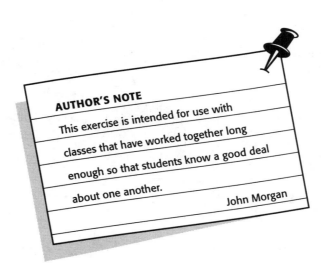

AUTHOR'S NOTE

This exercise is intended for use with classes that have worked together long enough so that students know a good deal about one another.

John Morgan

11 Feelings and Pictures

Level
High intermediate
and above

60

Language Functions
Expressing

Describing

Discussing feelings

MATERIALS	BEFORE CLASS
Reproductions of famous paintings in the form of slides, prints, postcards or on a computer; slide projector and screen (if slides are used)	Secure several reproductions of famous paintings and number each one.

1 Discuss with the class how words can express or describe emotions. Brainstorm vocabulary of emotions and feelings, and ask each student to write down words or expressions that he or she feels confident using or would like to experiment in using. Tell the class that you are going to give them the opportunity to use some of these words.

2 Display reproductions of several paintings. Use slides, a computer, prints or, as a last resort, postcards. The paintings should preferably be lesser-known works and/or works with ambiguous subject matter. Ask the students to write down their *feelings or impressions* as they see each painting. Be sure to allow adequate time for each picture.

3 Divide the class into small groups, and ask them to discuss their impressions and the vocabulary they have used to describe their feelings. Then ask each group to choose a picture and make up a title that sums up the group's feelings about it.

AUTHOR'S NOTE

As a variation, you may wish to ask students to mime the feelings they have collectively for a picture. Each group is to guess, from the mimes, the identity of the other group's pictures.

Marjorie Baudains

Intuiting a Picture

Level
Advanced

MATERIALS	BEFORE CLASS
Original or reproduction of an emotive painting or photograph	Select an emotive picture (a copy or a painting or an artistic photograph usually works well). Consider the kinds of feelings the picture arouses in you and the attitude to reality it conveys. Bring the picture to class.

Language Functions
Expressing feelings

Describing

1 Brainstorm general vocabulary about paintings with the class. Guide the brainstorming into the more specific area of your feelings about the painting, but avoid actually using words that directly express your feelings so as not to influence the students' own responses when they later see the picture.

2 Give the picture to one student without letting the others see it. Tell the student to describe the picture to the class, but to do so without mentioning anything in it. He or she must describe it purely in terms of the emotions it provokes. As the student describes the picture, have the rest of the class close their eyes and imagine a picture that fits the language they hear.

3 Then ask the students to discuss in pairs the kinds of pictures they imagined and make comparisons between them. Ask some of the students to describe their imagined pictures to the whole class.

4 Now show everyone the picture and ask for comments on it. Is it as they imagined it? Do they accept and agree with the first account of it in terms of feelings? Why or why not?

5 Finally, if the picture makes a specific point, it may be possible to start a discussion about that point.

Author
Randal Holme

13 Picking a Picture

Level
Intermediate and above

60

Language Functions
Expressing feelings

Explaining

Justifying

MATERIALS

Reproductions of twenty to thirty paintings, all periods and styles

BEFORE CLASS

Secure twenty to thirty reproductions of paintings of all periods and styles and number each one.

1 Lay the numbered pictures on a table, face up, and ask the students to each choose one they would like to talk about. Tell them they are not to reveal to you or the other students the picture they have chosen and they are not to remove it from the table.

2 Ask each student to write down, on his or her own paper, the names of the other students in the class. Next to each name students should then write the number of the picture they believe that student will have chosen.

3 Now ask the students to come up, one at a time, and take the picture they chose. They should tell the class about their feelings toward it and explain why they selected it. If more than one student has chosen the same picture, each may retrieve it from the one before and hold it up while explaining his or her choice.

4 After a particular student has explained his or her choice, the rest of the class should:
- say which picture they thought the student would choose, and why;
- give their own feelings about the picture that was chosen.

You may want to make a chart on the board for the first one.

5 Conduct a "debriefing" session in which you elicit discussion of the reasons for the differences in taste and the connections between the way people speak and behave and the kinds of art they select. Take care that this discussion is free of personal innuendo.

AUTHOR'S NOTE

This idea developed from seeing a demonstration of Randal Holme's "Intuiting a Picture" (Recipe 12).

David Hill

Creative Writing and Thinking

14 Identification Parade

Level
Low intermediate
and above

30–40

Language Functions
Describing

Identifying

MATERIALS
Portraits from magazines
Drawing paper
Paste
Tape

BEFORE CLASS

Cut out interesting portraits (photographs of ordinary people) from magazines. You'll need a portrait for each student in the class plus at least seven additional portraits. If possible, some of them, although of different people, should be similar in detail. Mount two of the portraits on large sheets of drawing paper so that vocabulary can be written around them. These two portraits should be full-page sized if possible, so that they can be seen by the whole class. Attach one of the mounted portraits to the wall (or board) so that it is clearly visible to all students.

Method One (with written responses)

1 Call attention to the mounted portrait, and start a discussion about it. Allow students to use as much vocabulary as possible to describe the portrait. As each term is introduced, write it, or have the person who introduced it write in on the paper surrounding the portrait. Help with any new words students are struggling to express. Depending on the level, you may wish to introduce new ways of talking about items like age, hair color, complexion, and so on. Add these to the words surrounding the portrait, but avoid turning the exercise into a glossary of new lexical terms. Include only words that you believe will be reused.

2 Now put up the second mounted portrait and repeat the process with it.

3 Explain to students that they are each going to receive a portrait of a person who is suspected of a petty crime such as shoplifting. The students are witnesses to the crime and must give an accurate description in writing of the person they saw commit the crime—that is, the person whose portrait they have. Then hand out the portraits, telling the students not to show their portrait to anyone else in the class. Give them time to write their descriptions. The descriptions should be on separate paper, *not* on the portraits.

4 When students have finished writing their descriptions, collect the pictures. Ask students to exchange descriptions so that each has the description written by another. Tell them to read their descriptions and think about the person described.

5 While students are reading the new descriptions, shuffle the portraits and add the remaining five. Lay the shuffled portraits on the table face up or put them up around the class. Then ask students to come up and identify the suspect based on the descriptions they have read. When they believe they have spotted the "right person," they should check with the writer of the description to make sure they are correct.

6 You may wish to take the activity one step further and ask students why they were so sure that the picture they chose was correct.

Method Two (no written responses)
Do Steps 1 and 2 as described in *Method One.* Then give portraits to half the students. These will be the witnesses. The other students will be detectives. Each witness will have a "detective" partner to whom he or she must give an oral description of the picture (obviously, the detective must not be able to see the picture). The detectives may take notes of the witnesses' descriptions and then, after the portraits have been collected, shuffled, and laid on the table or put up around the class (as in Step 5 of *Method One*), they must identify the suspects from the witnesses' descriptions.

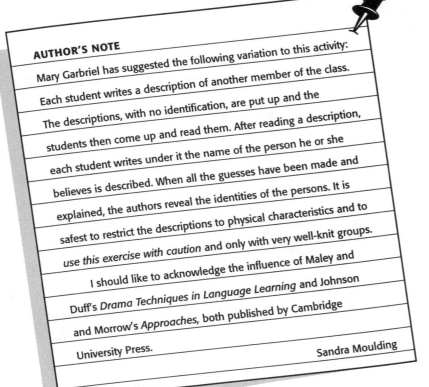

AUTHOR'S NOTE
Mary Garbriel has suggested the following variation to this activity: Each student writes a description of another member of the class. The descriptions, with no identification, are put up and the students then come up and read them. After reading a description, each student writes under it the name of the person he or she believes is described. When all the guesses have been made and explained, the authors reveal the identities of the persons. It is safest to restrict the descriptions to physical characteristics and to *use this exercise with caution* and only with very well-knit groups. I should like to acknowledge the influence of Maley and Duff's *Drama Techniques in Language Learning* and Johnson and Morrow's *Approaches*, both published by Cambridge University Press.

Sandra Moulding

Character Wheel 15

Level
Low intermediate and above

40

Language Functions
Imagining

Narrating

MATERIALS	BEFORE CLASS
Small pictures of people	Collect small pictures of people (one for each student). Mount each picture on a piece of blank writing paper.

1 Divide the class into groups of five to ten students and ask each group to form a circle. Distribute a picture to each student.

2 Now ask each student to give his or her picture a name, and write it on the paper under the picture. The student then passes the picture to the person on his or her right. This person adds the age and occupation, and again passes it to the student on the right. The following details are completed the same way, one being added by each student who passes it to the next student:

- marital status and size of family
- address
- hobbies and interests (one or two of each)
- one thing the person loves
- one thing the person hates

Keep the pace brisk and ask students to keep each contribution to one sentence. Give the class a few minutes to look at the completed sheets.

3 Now that the basic (imagined) facts about the people in the pictures have been stated, suggest that the class might try imagining following them around on a typical day in their lives. What did they do yesterday? Tell the class to write a narrative account in the simple past, beginning their first sentence with "Yesterday," and passing the pictures, this time to the left, after each student's contribution has been made. For this narrative, contributions should be limited to two sentences. The story for each character ends when the paper returns to the student who made the first contribution. (With very small groups and/or very eager students, you may wish to let the story make a second round.)

4 Let the students share the various accounts during the remainder of the class. At the end of class, collect the pictures and accounts; they can serve as the source of a list of common errors to be worked on in a later lesson.

5 A possible follow-up is to continue using the characters, building more and more information into their stories, perhaps even to the point of making them alter egos for the students.

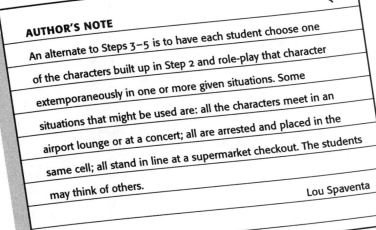

AUTHOR'S NOTE
An alternate to Steps 3–5 is to have each student choose one of the characters built up in Step 2 and role-play that character extemporaneously in one or more given situations. Some situations that might be used are: all the characters meet in an airport lounge or at a concert; all are arrested and placed in the same cell; all stand in line at a supermarket checkout. The students may think of others.

Lou Spaventa

16 Impressionistic Writing from Pictures

Level
Low intermediate
and above

45

Language Functions
Expressing feelings

Writing poetry

MATERIALS	BEFORE CLASS
An emotion-packed picture	Obtain a compelling picture (one that you believe will stir the emotions of the class). It may be strong and immediate or mysterious and elusive. It may be a reproduction of a painting or it may be a photograph. It should be large enough so that the whole class can see it when it is put up on the wall or board. Bring it to class but do not show it until Step 5.

1 Introduce the class to the idea of free writing—writing without thinking about the mechanics, such as punctuation or syntax. You might compare it to "free form" in abstract painting or perhaps to the "automatic writing" of a psychic.

2 Then write on the board the names of two or three emotions, such as anger, joy, hate, loneliness, love, jealousy. Be sure that your list includes some of the "negative" emotions; these often produce a more immediate response than the more positive ones. Tell the students they are going to "free-write" about emotions. They may choose those they wish to write about; ask them if there are others that should be added to the list on the board, and accept their suggestions.

3 Now write an impressionistic "poem" on the board, associating whatever words and phrases come into your head in connection with one or more of the emotions you have listed. The train of association will produce words and images that are disconnected. These should be laid out on the board in lines as in a free verse poem.

4 Now ask the students to write a "poem" of their own as you have done. (It does not matter if your poem influences those of the students. It is essential that you write one first to give the class confidence and to show them the kind of thing they are to do; it also forms a relationship between you and the class. Nor does the teacher's poem inhibit the class at all.) After a minute or two, erase your poem while the students continue to write their own.

5 Now introduce the class to the picture you have brought. Ask them to write about it in just the same way they have written about the "emotion words." Encourage the students, but do not pressure them. Tell them that it does not matter how they begin, and that once the first few words are on paper, things usually seem to flow. Urge them to use words that express what the picture means to them. Tell them you are going to be writing your own poem while they are writing theirs.

6 Write your own poem, either on paper or on the board. If you write on the board, wait until students are well into their own work first.

7 Have students read their poems and discuss them, comparing the different meanings they found in the picture. Finally, collect the poems into an anthology and photocopy it for the students. Keep a copy of the anthology to show to people who tell you it can't be done!

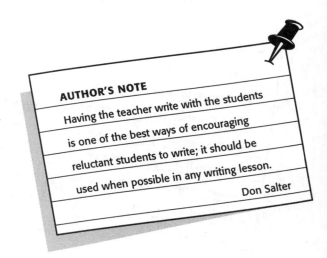

AUTHOR'S NOTE

Having the teacher write with the students is one of the best ways of encouraging reluctant students to write; it should be used when possible in any writing lesson.

Don Salter

Advertisements 17

Level
Low intermediate
and above

15–
30

Language Function
Persuading

MATERIALS	BEFORE CLASS
Magazines and/or newspapers Optional: audio or video (recording) equipment.	Cut out the following from magazines and/or newspapers: • Advertisements • Headlines from advertisements • Pictures of various kinds

1 Give each student a copy of a magazine advertisement. Ask the students to comment on what is being sold and on how the advertisement tries to catch the reader's eye and persuade him or her to buy.

2 Then give each student a headline from another advertisement. Avoid duplication; each student should have a separate headline to work with, different from those of the other students.

3 Put the pictures face up on the table and let each student choose one that he or she can relate to the headline, thus creating an advertisement.

4 Give the students about ten minutes to complete their ads, writing further copy as needed and practicing reading their ads orally for a presentation (lower levels may require more time). As students work, move around the room acting as language consultant but not as idea person. A thesaurus and a few dictionaries strategically placed will help deflect many of the vocabulary questions.

5 When the students have finished, ask them, one at a time, to read their advertisements in an expressive, persuasive, and entertaining manner, trying to attract and interest the listeners. If possible, record the students (audio or video) as they make their presentations. The recordings can then be played back, first straight through and then with pauses to give the group an opportunity to comment on what they hear.

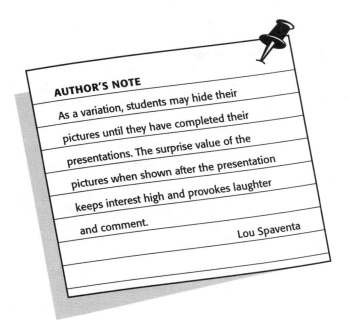

AUTHOR'S NOTE

As a variation, students may hide their pictures until they have completed their presentations. The surprise value of the pictures when shown after the presentation keeps interest high and provokes laughter and comment.

Lou Spaventa

18 Imaging

Level
Low intermediate
and above

30

Language Function
Making suggestions
and associations

MATERIALS	BEFORE CLASS
Small object(s) for which uses are to be imagined	Collect a variety of small objects.

1 Present a simple, everyday object such as a cake tin, a large envelope, or a paper clip. Tell the class that they are to think of as many uses as possible for the object. A rectangular cake tin, for example, could be used for storing pencils or other small objects, but you could also put wheels on it and use it for a skateboard (as suggested by one student for a metal candy box). The more imaginative responses the better. It is important not to reject any ideas/proposals—to do so could block other suggestions that students might have.

2 The students can work individually, in pairs, or in small groups. Give them a few minutes to think and discuss, and then go around the class, collecting their contributions. Ask students to explain their uses if necessary, but try not to interrupt the rhythm. Encourage them to use structures like "It could (might) be used as a . . ." but do not interrupt if students' imaginations are working productively.

3 Next have the class do a word association, either with the name of the original object or with one of the words that has come up frequently in the discussion of uses. Ask students to give as many associations as they can with the key word. Accept all associations even if they seem remote; the purpose is to generate imaginative associations.

4 Now select a word that has come up in Step 2. It should be something concrete and easy to visualize. For example, if the original object was an envelope, an appropriate word might be "stamp" (if envelopes had been suggested for storing stamps). Tell the students to close their eyes and form a picture in their minds of the word you have chosen. Tell them to picture it within a frame or on a screen but to imagine it is moving within that area.

5 Ask a member of the class to describe what he or she is visualizing. Then move to another student, asking him or her to continue, then another student, and so on, to build up a group fantasy. Prompt as necessary with questions such as, "What color is it?", "What's happening?", "What does it look like now?", "Has it changed?", or "What is it doing now?" Emphasize the visual aspect in your questions; you want the student to tell you what he or she is "seeing."

6 A useful variation for Steps 1 and 2 is to hold an initial group session with the entire class and then divide the group into pairs. Let them continue suggesting uses to each other, taking turns as in a game, with the rule that each one can stop the other by simply saying "Stop!" and then making his or her own contributions.

7 Finally, return to the original object you brought in and rethink possible uses of it.

8 For more advanced classes, an interesting follow-up is to investigate the whole issue of convergent and divergent thinking. A reference librarian can direct you to sources; one such is *Contrary Imaginations* by Liam Hudson (Pelican). Another is *The Nature of Human Intelligence* by J.P. Guilford (McGraw-Hill). Students might be interested in investigating such questions as how convergent and divergent thinking vary with persons of different ages, sexes, and occupations, divergent thinking's relation to creativity, and its susceptibility to development.

AUTHOR'S NOTE

I understand that this technique has been widely used in group work to facilitate creative attempts at problem solving, but I do not know the exact origin.

Chris Sion

Anecdote Analysis 19

Level
Low intermediate
and above

Language Functions
Narrating

Combining items
of information

MATERIALS	BEFORE CLASS
None	Requires no preparation!

1 Work with the class to create a story. The story can be based on anything: an amusing incident, something that has happened to the students in using their English, a few unrelated pictures, a book, etc. Encourage each student to make a contribution so that all of them can feel that it is their story. You may wish to write it on the board so that everybody can see it as it is constructed, or you may write it in a notebook as the students dictate it to you.

2 Before the next class, condense the story into about twelve sentences and type or print each sentence on a separate strip of paper. This is a good place to introduce new words; the students are likely to remember them because they are in "their" story. Make sure that the sentences include something from every member of the group and that there are enough strips so that each student will have one.

3 At the next session pass out the strips, making sure that everybody gets at least one. Then ask the class to put the story together in sequence. Provide help only if there is a serious problem.

4 Once the sentences are in the correct order, ask individual students to dictate the story to you and write it on the board. Hesitate obviously at garbled pronunciation and encourage the rest of the class to help in making you understand what to write. Allow time for those who want to copy the story themselves.

AUTHOR'S NOTE

There will probably be many verbs in the simple past, comparatives, and/or relative pronouns in the story. The exercise provides an opportunity to analyze and discuss these. Ask the students to tell you the words to write on the board for this purpose. You can also have them list regular past endings, put irregular verbs into their logical groupings, and cover other related points the class may have missed.

Mike Perry

20 Do-It-Yourself Comprehension

Level
Low intermediate
and above

30

Language Functions
Narrating

Answering questions

MATERIALS

Photocopies of the questions (and the text) may be used but are not essential

BEFORE CLASS

Prepare about ten comprehension questions similar to those used in standard comprehension tests. They can be based either on an existing passage from a textbook or on a passage that does not actually exist. Bring in whatever structures and vocabulary you wish to practice or reinforce. Upgrade or downgrade the questions to suit the level of the class. Photocopy the questions if you decide to present them in this way (see Step 2). You should also make the necessary photocopies if you have based your questions on a text and want to distribute copies of it (see Step 4).

An example of a set of questions not based on a text but simply made up is as follows:

1 Why was David so exhausted when he got back to the village?

2 Was he surprised to find the village deserted? Why or why not?

3 The writer suggests three possible reasons why the village had been abandoned. Write two of them.

4 What did David discover on opening the front door of his cottage?

5 What would you have done in these circumstances? What did David do?

6 Which of the girls was real and which was a figment of David's imagination?

7 What led David to the realization that something was wrong?

8 Do you think he was justified in being so violent? Why or why not?

9 How many survivors were discovered before dawn? What was done with the remains of those who did not survive?

10 What would be a good title for the passage you have written?

1 Review with students the standard comprehension exercise technique in which they read a passage and then answer questions about it. If you have used exercises of this kind recently, you may wish to remind them of specific passages and questions. Tell them that they are going to do a variation of this technique this time. In fact, they are going to do such an exercise backwards.

2 Present the questions you have prepared to the students. You can either write them on the board or pass out copies of them. Tell the students that this time they are not to answer the questions but instead they are to write a passage on which the questions could be based. They must be sure that every question can be answered by reading the passage they write. (This allows the students to use their imagination within a framework set by you.)

3 When the passages have been completed, have students read them aloud. You will probably find as many striking similarities as you will differences. Let the class discuss and compare the passages they have written.

4 Finally, if you have based your questions on a real passage, present this to the class either by reading it aloud, putting it on the board, or passing out copies. Discuss how the students' passages compare with the original. If you did not base your questions on an actual passage, this is the time to say so.

AUTHOR'S NOTE

I have found that there is sometimes a terrible anti-climax when the class is finally told that there isn't really a passage at all. It seems important not to actually lie to them when you present the instructions and questions.

Jean-Paul Creton

What Should We Talk About?

Level
Low intermediate
and above

40–50 • **2** DAYS • 20–30

Language Functions
Exchanging ideas

Reporting

Narrating

MATERIALS	BEFORE CLASS
None	Requires no preparation!

1 Start a discussion about students' interests. Then ask each student to write three topics of interest on a piece of paper.

2 Divide the class into pairs, and ask each pair to discuss their lists and look for similarities. Then ask the pairs to join together to make groups of four. They should again discuss their lists. Circulate among the groups, noting popular topics.

3 Now ask a spokesperson for each group to tell the class the interests of that group. Following this, ask students, on the basis of these reports, to form new "interest-based" topic groups. Let them circulate freely and question others in order to find the group they want to join. You may end up with three or four definite interest groups. "Strays" should be urged to join one or another of the groups, whichever comes nearest to touching on their interest.

4 Tell the groups that they are to use the remainder of the period to prepare an introductory talk on the subject for a later class. Let the groups choose when they would like to give their talks, and arbitrate any schedule conflicts.

5 When the scheduled time comes, have the groups present their talks. Do not let one student dominate the proceedings, however; be sure that each one has the opportunity to speak. The discussion can continue with the whole class asking questions and making contributions and a student from any one of the groups taking the chair.

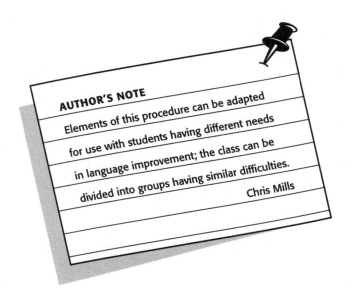

AUTHOR'S NOTE

Elements of this procedure can be adapted for use with students having different needs in language improvement; the class can be divided into groups having similar difficulties.

Chris Mills

Reading and Writing

22 Headlines

Level
Intermediate and above

50

Language Functions
Interpreting

Suggesting

MATERIALS

Newspaper articles
(including headlines)

Paste

Envelopes

BEFORE CLASS

Select newspaper articles with headlines appropriate to the level of your class. You will need about three articles for each of the small groups into which you divide the class (Step 1).

Cut the headlines off the articles and cut each headline into separate words. You may want to mount each article and each headline word on paper. This makes for easier handling and also ensures that students are seeing the correct side of the cut-out piece of newspaper and are not confused by what happens to be on the back. (For the purposes of the exercise it is preferable that all headlines be in the same type size and style.)

Shuffle the words in the three headlines for each group and put them in envelopes so that all the words for the first group are in one envelope, those for the second group are in another, and so on.

1 Divide the class into small groups, and pass out the envelopes of shuffled headline words.

2 Tell each group that their envelopes contain words from three headlines. They are to reconstruct the headlines by putting the right words together. Tell them that you will provide the literal meaning of any words they don't understand but point out that headlines do not always use words in their literal sense; students must work out any metaphorical meanings for themselves.

3 Let the groups work for as long as necessary. Provide help where you think it is needed. Assembling the headlines should take about ten minutes, although this will vary with the level of the class.

4 When the headlines have been assembled, ask each group to read its headlines and tell what they mean and what the group feels the article was about. Then ask each student to take one of the headlines and write his or her own version of an article to go with that headline. (If there are more students than headlines, some can copy the headline and work from the copy.) The articles should be short, perhaps five to twelve sentences.

5 Have the students read their articles to the class. Finally, students can compare their versions with the original articles from the newspaper.

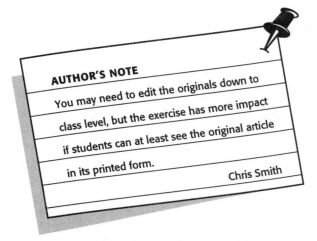

AUTHOR'S NOTE

You may need to edit the originals down to class level, but the exercise has more impact if students can at least see the original article in its printed form.

Chris Smith

Dear Ann Landers 23

Level
Intermediate

45

Language Functions
Discussing problems and solutions to problems

Replying to letters

MATERIALS	BEFORE CLASS
Letters and replies from typical, personal advice columns Index cards Paste	Cut out several letters and their replies from typical advice columns such as "Dear Abby" or "Ann Landers." Paste them on index cards, with a letter on one side of the card and the answer to a different letter on the other side. For example, the answer to letter "A" may appear on the back of letter "C," and so on. However, the entire set will include all the letters and their answers.

1

Method One

Have a student read one of the letters to the class. The class discusses the problem and suggests solutions. After a couple of letters have been read and discussed, the students look at the backs of the cards for the columnist's answer and discuss that, comparing it with their own replies.

Method Two

As an alternate, ask each student to write a reply to a letter that has been read to the class. Or give each student one of the letters and ask him or her to draft a reply to it. In either case, compare the student reply with the columnist's answer.

Method Three

(This can be used either as an alternative to *Method One* and *Method Two* or as a follow-up to either.) Give each student a reply and ask him or her to write a letter in response to the reply. Then ask students to look through the cards and find the original letter. (If this method is used as a follow-up, be sure that the responses used are not among those already seen by the class.)

2

After the students have completed the exercise with the letters, lead a discussion on related topics such as loneliness in the modern world, communication breakdowns between people, or what leads men and women to write to advice columns of this kind.

AUTHOR'S NOTE

If your students are teenagers or young people in their early twenties, you may wish to use a column directed specifically toward young people. "Ask Beth" is one such syndicated column in the United States. However, both Abigail VanBuren ("Dear Abby") and Ann Landers include letters from young people as well as those from older adults, and their columns, because of wider syndication, may be easier to find.

Mike Levy

Handwriting

Level
Intermediate

30–
40

Language Functions
Speculating

Describing

Comparing

MATERIALS	BEFORE CLASS
Two letters written in different scripts Pictures of people	You need two handwritten letters, one of which is a reply to the other. The letters should be very different in style and written in very different scripts. The letters should be one or two pages in length so that students can easily read them. Also collect several pictures of people to distribute after Step 3 is completed.

1 Pass around the two letters. If you can make photocopies, this will speed the exercise, but make sure that you also have the originals so that students see that these are real letters. Allow time for each student to read both letters.

2 Discuss the content of the letters and the background of the situation in which they were written. (If they were written "to order" for you, you will need to invent a plausible background for them.)

3 Now have the class describe the people who wrote the letters. Elicit a general personal description together with details of the writers' lifestyles. The different handwritings and the variations in literary style provide powerful stimuli for imagining what the writers are like.

4 Distribute pictures of people to serve as additional (or alternative) stimuli, and ask the students, perhaps working in pairs, to say which two people the correspondence might have been between and to explain the reasons for their choices.

5 As a follow-up, have each student write a handwritten reply to the second letter. (This is a good exercise for homework, and you may wish to correct their letters as you would other homework exercises.) At the next session, return the letters to the students, divide the class into small groups, and ask them to compare their styles of writing and their scripts. Do they have any memories of learning to write? Do their varying scripts say anything about themselves? You might suggest that students take a look at a handwriting analysis website; one such site is www.handwriting.org.

Author
Cynthia Beresford

Text Messages 25

Level
Intermediate and above

60

Language Functions
Sending and interpreting
text messages

Writing letters and e-mails

Using the phone

MATERIALS

Examples of text messages,
one per student

BEFORE CLASS

Prepare a set of typical text messages that could be sent from a cell
phone. You need one for each student. Each message should be on
a separate piece of paper. Some examples of the kind of messages
you might include are:

A AM OUT EARLY TODAY. CAN YOU MEET ME
DOWNTOWN FOR LUNCH? XXX, KIM

B UNCLE BILL IN HOSPITAL. CONDITION STABLE.
TERRIBLY SORRY BUT HE'LL BE OK. TAKE CARE, MARIA

C PLEASE SEND MONEY. PASSPORT STOLEN. AM IN
LOCAL POLICE STATION. THANKS, JOHN

D HAVE BROKEN LEG. CANCEL TICKETS. BEST, KEN

1 Review with the class the form and use of text messages as compared with those of letters, e-mails, and
the telephone.

2 Divide the class into pairs and give each student one
of the text messages you have prepared. You may
give out more than one copy of a particular message but
each pair of students should have two different messages.

3 Working together, partners should decide what the
relationship is between sender and recipient for
each of their two text messages. Partners then choose
one of the messages and write a letter to the recipient,
expanding on the content.

4 Collect the letters, work with the students on their
errors, and then pass the letters around the class.
The letters should be accompanied by the text messages
on which they were based.

5 Ask each pair of students to improvise a phone
conversation between the sender and the recipient
of the other text message.

6 Have the improvised phone conversations
performed as dialogues. Before each dialogue,
one member of each pair should read out the message
on which it was based.

Variations

A Students in class can answer the letters.

B Students who have computers can respond to the
letters by e-mail as a homework assignment. Arrange
in class who is going to send whom an e-mail
concerning which message.

C Students write a text message or e-mail on a particular
subject using only a limited number of words.

Author
Marjorie Baudains

Extensive Reading

Level
Advanced

40

Language Functions
Extracting information from written texts

Scanning

Asking and answering questions

MATERIALS	BEFORE CLASS
A newspaper	Prepare newspaper pages for each member of the class. Be sure that each page has two or more complete articles on it.

1 Give one newspaper page to each member of the class.

2 Tell students that they are to read one of the articles on their page and then, on the board, write a question about that article. They are not to identify the article on which the question is based. The question should be such that it can be answered only by reading the article. When each student has written his or her question, they are to return the newspaper page to you.

3 Spread all the newspaper pages around the class in random order. Then ask students to find the answers to the questions on the board. This will require quick,

efficient reading of the material. After they have located the relevant article, students should scan the article to find the answer to the question. Ideally, let the students circulate around the room. If this isn't possible in your teaching situation, the pages will have to be passed around the class.

4 Go through the answers with the class as soon as the first person has finished. If you wish, you may discuss with the students the kind of reasoning they used to locate the correct articles.

Author
Paul Cammack

Appreciating Advertisements

Level
Intermediate and above

Language Functions
Explaining and
justifying choices

Describing

MATERIALS	BEFORE CLASS
Magazines	Requires no preparation!

1 Bring a pile of magazines into class and tell the students to spend the next fifteen minutes leafing through them, looking especially at the advertisements.

2 Now tell the students to select some or all of the following:
   A   an advertisement they like
   B   an advertisement they hate
   C   an advertisement they think is good
   D   an advertisement they think is bad

3 Go around the class, asking each student to describe and discuss one of the advertisements he or she has chosen. Students should explain and justify their choices. Encourage questions and comments from the rest of the class.

4 On the board, write any advertising slogans, catch phrases, or other details you may wish to draw attention to; these items should flow out of points brought up in Step 3. Discuss these with the class, calling for examples from some of the selected ads.

Author
David Hill

Ambiguity in Advertising

Level
Intermediate and above

45

Language Functions
Detecting ambiguity

Interpreting figurative
language

Interpreting non-verbal
graphic cues

Recognizing connotative
and denotative meanings

MATERIALS

Magazines with advertise-
ments or advertisements
cut from magazines

BEFORE CLASS

Cut out and mount several advertisements containing slogans that
have double meanings. For more advanced groups, bring in old
magazines from which the students can select such ads.

1 Pass out the advertisements to the class and analyze
the double meanings in the slogans or headlines.
(With more advanced classes you may have students
locate such advertisements in old magazines. They can
work in pairs, in small groups, or as a whole class.)

2 Discuss the reasons that advertisers use the
language they do. Why, for example, would an
advertiser for jeans coin and use the phrase, "We've
given your waist a little squeeze!"?

3 Ask the students to analyze other factors (apart from
slogans) that advertisers use to catch the eye. For
example, how are the subjects positioned? What is the
layout like? How are the connotations (associated meanings) of words used in contrast to their denotations?
What is the target audience of a particular ad? What social
class, age, generation, or sex is being appealed to, and
how does the student know this? How are stereotypes
made use of? At which unconscious areas of the personality is the ad directed? How does the student know?

Author
Chris Mills

The Misuse of Words 29

Level
Advanced

60

Language Function
Appreciating syntax

MATERIALS	BEFORE CLASS
Newspapers or magazines	Select magazine and/or newspaper pages that contain articles your students can understand. You'll need one page for each student.

1 Give each student one of the pages you have selected. The pages need not be the same.

2 Ask each student to select an article from his or her page–preferably something of personal interest. Each student should then pick one or two sentences from the page. Any sentences will do, but the total number of words should not exceed twenty-five. Explain any unknown vocabulary.

3 Ask each student to take out a blank piece of paper and write their sentences in *vertical* columns of five words with adequate spacing between both the words and the columns.

For example, the sentences: "'We have other inquiries going on,' a police officer said. Early reports had said that police were looking for heroin and cocaine." should be written:

WE	ON	EARLY	POLICE	AND
HAVE	A	REPORTS	WERE	COCAINE
OTHER	POLICE	HAD	LOOKING	
INQUIRIES	OFFICER	SAID	FOR	
GOING	SAID	THAT	HEROIN	

4 Collect the sheets of paper. Redistribute them, making sure that no student receives his or her own sheet. Now ask the students to make new sentences using the columns of words.

They should now work *horizontally* and add words of their own as in the example below. The sentences may be any length but must be grammatically and syntactically correct.

WE were	ON the road	EARLY but the	POLICE noticed us	AND stopped us. We
HAVE always given them	A look at our	REPORTS which	WERE about	COCAINE and
OTHER substances of interest to the	POLICE. We	HAD been	LOOKING for heroin and making	
INQUIRIES about it.	An OFFICER	SAID he had searched	FOR years,	
GOING all over the country.	He SAID also	THAT they were sure	HEROIN was being sold here.	

Author
Marjorie Baudains

Graphic Experiences

Level
High Intermediate
and above

45–60

Language Function
Identifying emotions

MATERIALS	BEFORE CLASS
Audio equipment with a recorded dialogue or video equipment with a short video sequence	Select an audio recording or video sequence of two people talking. The language should have strong emotional impact.

1 Tell students you are going to play them a short dialogue; you may wish to brief them on the content. Play the dialogue once. Ask students to identify the characters: Who are they? What is their relationship? Where are they? Then ask the class to discuss what the characters are feeling and why. This is perhaps best done in pairs or small groups.

2 Tell students that you are going to play the recording again and that their task is to draw a graph of what they hear. Ask them to take out a piece of paper and a pen and to draw two axes in preparation for the "graphic experience." Help by drawing on the board a horizontal and vertical axis similar to this:

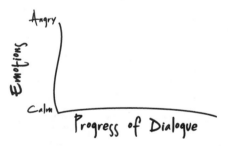

Tell students to chart the emotions of *both* characters, perhaps using different colors. Warn them that they might not be able to keep up with the dialogue but that you will play it several times if necessary, so they should just relax and include as much as they can. Then play the recording and allow the students to draw their graphs as described.

3 Divide the class into pairs again and ask the students to swap their graphs and explain what they have drawn. This should force them to recall the language used in the dialogue, for example: "This is where the woman screams that she can't go on."

4 Play the recording again, this time asking the students to write some of the key phrases on their graphs. This can be done in pairs or as an individual exercise. Don't hesitate to replay the recording if the class needs to hear it again. Then invite one student (or pair) to the front to draw his or her representation on the board and fill in the language at the key points. Discuss this with the class, inviting comparisons, or if necessary, corrections. When analyzing the language, pay particular attention to the intonation and register patterns found in the dialogue.

5 Follow up by giving students a list of sentences for intonation practice. Some productive examples are:

- I'll always love you.
- I'll do it tomorrow.
- I don't think so.
- I thought I left it here.
- Do you really?

Ask students to recite the sentences aloud, using what they think is the correct intonation (i.e., anger, threat, or persuasion) for whichever emotions are represented in the graph. Encourage students to repeat their efforts several times. Finally, divide the class into pairs to simulate a situation where one or two of these sentences are used in a particular and deliberate functional way, such as to express disagreement.

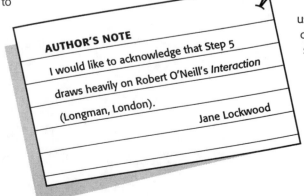

AUTHOR'S NOTE

I would like to acknowledge that Step 5 draws heavily on Robert O'Neill's *Interaction* (Longman, London).

Jane Lockwood

Inner Listening 31

Level
Intermediate and above

30

Language Functions
Making associations

Narrating

Asking questions

MATERIALS

Recording of a piece of music with audio equipment or a musical instrument

BEFORE CLASS

Choose a short piece of music that is without words and is appropriate to your group. You will either have to obtain a recorded version of it or be prepared to play it on the guitar, piano, or other instrument.

1 Ask the class to listen to the music quietly as you play it for them once. Then ask students to jot down all the thoughts, images, and feelings that go through their heads while you play the music a second time. Tell them to write freely, without worrying about grammar or organization.

2 Tell students to connect their notes and turn them into a story. Let them hear the music again as they write.

3 Divide the class into pairs and ask students to discuss the development of their notes into stories. They should focus on the progression from thoughts, associations, and feelings into stories. They should listen closely and be able to satisfactorily repeat their partner's account.

4 Ask *one student from each pair* to leave the room. The rest of the students should stay in the classroom. *Both groups* of students should select new partners. Using the first story, each pair should recount the stories they have just heard to their new partners. In other words, they should retell their original partner's story as if it were their own.

5 Bring the class back together. Each person must find his or her original story by questioning the others, who relate the *second* story they were told. This exercise ends when discovery is complete. You may wish to round things off with a final playing of the music.

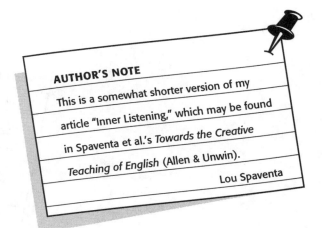

AUTHOR'S NOTE

This is a somewhat shorter version of my article "Inner Listening," which may be found in Spaventa et al.'s *Towards the Creative Teaching of English* (Allen & Unwin).

Lou Spaventa

Unintentional Listening

Level
All

20–30

Language Function
Combining items
of information

MATERIALS	BEFORE CLASS
Audio equipment Recording of a song Construction paper	Select a song that relates to the level and interests of your class. It is not important if the class knows the music, but they should not be conversant with the lyrics, and the song should not be too long. Write the words of the song, line by line, on construction paper; make enough copies so that there will be one for about every three students. Then cut up the copies so that each line of the song is on a separate strip. Shuffle the strips for each set.

1 Divide the class into groups of three and distribute one of the cut-up paper sets to each group. Their task is to sort them into the correct order. New vocabulary can be pre-taught or explained as problems arise.

2 When the students are busily sorting out the strips, start playing the song you have selected; it should initially be *too soft to hear.* Keep replaying it, gradually increasing the volume, but without attracting attention to yourself. The exercise works best when sorting out the lines proves a little too difficult for the group and the music becomes clearly audible just as the students' attention is beginning to wander. They suddenly realize that if they listen, they *can* find the words.

3 When the groups have all finished sorting the lines, collect the sets of strips so you can use them again. If possible, give the class a handout of the complete lyrics. Otherwise write the lyrics on the board (perhaps with the students dictating to you), and then let the class write them down so that they have a written record of the song. Explain anything that is not altogether clear, answer questions, and finally sing the song together as a class, perhaps allowing one of the students to take the lead.

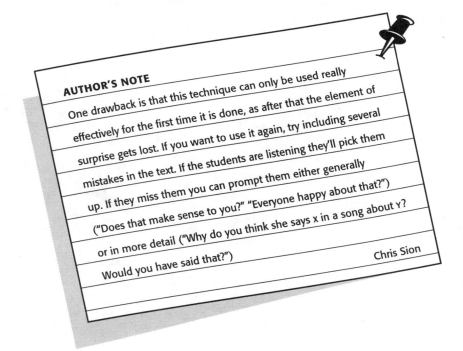

AUTHOR'S NOTE

One drawback is that this technique can only be used really effectively for the first time it is done, as after that the element of surprise gets lost. If you want to use it again, try including several mistakes in the text. If the students are listening they'll pick them up. If they miss them you can prompt them either generally ("Does that make sense to you?" "Everyone happy about that?") or in more detail ("Why do you think she says x in a song about y? Would you have said that?")

Chris Sion

Expanding on Songs 33

Level
Intermediate

 30–60

Language Functions
Narrating

Describing

Comparing

MATERIALS

Audio equipment and recording of a suitable song

BEFORE CLASS

Select the song you are going to use. I have chosen the "Unhappy Housewife" song from Abbs and Freebairn's *Strategies* (Longman, London). The song is recorded on *Skyhigh,* the accompanying tape. Many other narrative songs could be used in the same way.

1 Teach the class the song so that they know it thoroughly. Divide the class into pairs and ask them to tell about the song they heard. When they are finished, ask them to comment on the song. In the case of "The Unhappy Housewife," students would discuss what has happened and where they think the woman is going and what sort of reception she is going to have. (The song deals with a housewife who finally walks out on the man whose housework she has faithfully done for years.) Ask the pairs to report back to the class.

2 Now ask students to visualize the characters and describe them, their general background and way of life, hopes and fears, likes and dislikes, in as much detail as interest allows. A variation is to distribute aspects of the description among the class. One pair works on the description of the man, another on the woman, a third on their house, the family or the man's job, and so on. Then students swap notes and try to reach agreement on a coherent class picture of the characters and their background.

3 Set up a role-play of the situation. This should include roles for friends and other members of the family, a marriage counselor, perhaps even the milkman! But remember that this is dangerous territory and could prove extremely painful to a class member who has (or whose parents have) actually separated. You might continue by switching the students around and letting them play several different roles, but do not allow the activity to become boring by going on too long.

4 Step 3 can lead to a discussion on the roles of men and women, wives and husbands, or of cultural differences and role definitions. Another follow-up exercise is for students to write a further verse for the song, or even a new song giving the husband's point of view. Or the students could make up letters from estranged couples to practice a wide range of styles—for example heartbroken, threatening, cold, formal, pre-divorce, or wanting to make up. If interest permits, the students could finally be asked to reply to one of the others' letters. It goes without saying that not *all* these ideas should always be used. Try discussing them with your class and letting them decide what they want to do.

AUTHOR'S NOTE

This recipe deals specifically with one particular song. Many other songs, for example "She's Leaving Home" by The Beatles, could be used in a similar way by adapting the instructions to the content.

David Sanders

34 My Leader Is Brave

Level
Intermediate

15

Language Function
Asking questions

MATERIALS	BEFORE CLASS
None	Requires no preparation!

Method One

1 Explain to students that the class is going on an imaginary expedition. Students must try to establish what they may take with them by asking questions. For example: "May I take my shoes?" "Can Mary take her camera?" Ask students to write down a few questions to get them going. Once the exercise is underway there should be plenty of spontaneous questions.

2 Answer simply "Yes" or "No" according to the following system. *Roberto* can take a *ring*, a *rug*, some *rice*—anything that begins with the letter "r" as his name does. Similarly, *Cathy* can take *cake*, *cola*, *cornflakes* and so on, but not root bear, asparagus, bananas or tofu.

3 Encourage the class to dredge up as many words as they can so as to yield a lot of vocabulary. The students who manage to grasp the system should *not* tell the others. Instead, get them to take over your role in answering the questions.

Method Two

This is a more complex version, which is based on both initials and can be used to practice the passive. Begin with yourself and your "ship." A sentence based on *Mike Lavery* might be: "My ship is powered by *m*armalade and sinks with *l*emonade." Go on to single out the students, saying to *Alberto Bender*, for example: "Alberto, your ship is powered by *a*pples and sinks with *b*ottles." The students may ask questions to try and find out about their own (and their classmates') ships. They should not let on if they crack the code, but should simply join in, making statements about themselves and others. This allows you to fade into the background gradually until total student-student interaction has been established. Only intervene if there is a lapse in the exchanges.

Method Three

If you want to bring in a still more complicated dimension, base the vocabulary on the initials of a person sitting on a given person's left or right.

AUTHORS' NOTE

The key to this activity lies in using the students' initials to generate vocabulary. It is therefore imperative that everyone knows each others' names. No prizes for decoding the title!

Mike Lavery

Ian Butcher

Sounds Different

MATERIALS	BEFORE CLASS
Cards (see *Before Class*)	Find or prepare cards with an illustration on one side and, ideally, the relevant word written on the other, with contrasts such as "bear/beer" or "pen/pan." Sharron Bassano's *Sounds Easy!* (Alta Book Center Publishers) has some excellent examples you can photocopy and put to immediate use. Select the pairs of pictures you want to use.

Level
Intermediate

20–30

Language Function
Identifying and practicing sounds

1 Show students the illustrated side of the cards one by one and ask them to identify the objects pictured. Elicit the vocabulary from the group as much as possible, prompting as necessary. Write the words in two numbered columns on the board on the basis of contrasting sounds. For example:

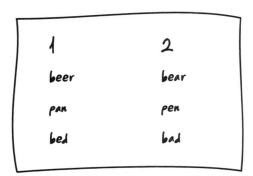

2 Say one of the words without indicating how it is spelled. The students have to decide which column on the board it comes from and should repeat the word. If they get the wrong column they must repeat both parts of the minimal pair. For example: "ship/sheep."

3 Ask students to call out words from the columns while the teacher or other students indicate which words they think are being said. Again, if the word has not been pronounced correctly, *both* parts of the minimal pair must be repeated.

Variations

A Give a sentence incorporating one of the relevant words and have students choose which is correct, for example: "Yesterday I went for a ride in a *ship/sheep*," or "I had a *beer/bear* with my dinner." Ask the class to make sentences in the same way.

B Put some of the cards in various places around the class and ask questions like "Where is the *bear?*" or "Is the *pan* on the table?"

C Divide the class into teams. Divide the cards equally between the teams and tell them to write a short story containing all the words on their cards. Be sure to check that the stories are in correct English. This can give you valuable insight into many other areas that need to be dealt with as a basis for future work. When they are ready, each group selects a spokesperson who reads the story to the rest of the class. Illustrate it on the board, pretending to misunderstand words that are incorrectly pronounced, so that the students have to emphasize. For example: "No, not ship; *sheep.*" This will show that they have genuinely grasped the difference.

Author
Mike Levy

36 Extensive/Intensive Listening

Level
Low intermediate
and above

30–40

Language Function
Asking and answering
factual questions

MATERIALS	BEFORE CLASS
Two recorded copies of a short news item or similar material Two sets of audio equipment If possible, two rooms	Record something from the radio, for example an interesting news item, which is not too long but is at a level challenging to the class. Make an additional copy of it so that you can use it with both groups when you split the class in two.

1 Divide the class into two groups. If possible, arrange to have the groups in separate rooms. Give each group their audio equipment and a copy of the recording. Tell them to listen to it and then prepare questions about the material for the other group. Set a time limit. Circulate, keeping an eye on what the students are doing, but letting them organize themselves as much as possible.

2 Have students re-assemble as one class. The groups should ask each other their questions while a "secretary" for each group writes down the answers. It is probably best to start by having each group ask one

question of the other group so that the students from both groups are discussing their answers simultaneously. This working "in parallel" is most effective and is not difficult to organize. Make sure that students take turns at asking the questions; do not let one or two of them monopolize the activity.

3 Finally, replay the recording to the whole class. The students should check to be sure that their answers are correct. Draw attention to any inaccuracies they might have overlooked.

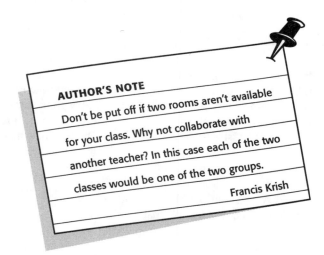

AUTHOR'S NOTE

Don't be put off if two rooms aren't available for your class. Why not collaborate with another teacher? In this case each of the two classes would be one of the two groups.

Francis Krish

Aural Comprehension

MATERIALS	BEFORE CLASS
Short recorded text or dialogue Audio equipment	Choose a fairly short recorded text suitable to the needs and interests of your class.

Level
Intermediate and above

Language Function
Notetaking

1 Tell students in one or two sentences what the recording is about and then play it through once. Do not tell the class to look for any particular elements.

2 Tell students that you are going to play the recording again and this time they should take notes as they listen to it. Give them a minute or two to get out their writing materials and then play the recording through again from beginning to end without stopping, even if there are questions.

3 Divide the class into groups of three or four students. Their task is to compare their notes and discuss what they think the main points of the text were. Ask each group to elect a "secretary" to make a written summary. Circulate, answering any questions, helping as necessary, and making sure that the interaction is in English.

4 Ask each group to elect a spokesperson to read, or, if possible, tell the class without reading verbatim, what they have written. The rest of the class should listen carefully and draw attention to any errors in the content or the language, perhaps by tapping on the desk with a pencil, or shouting out "Stop!" or "Challenge!"

5 While this is going on, write on the board (drawing as little attention to yourself as you can so as not to interrupt) any factually or grammatically incorrect sentences the students have overlooked. Only when the groups have all given their accounts should the students' attention be turned to the material on the board and the class asked to correct the error, without your help wherever possible. Finish off with a final playing of the recording.

Author
Sonia Taylor

38 Notetaking and a Story

Level
Low intermediate
and above

40

Language Function
Notetaking

MATERIALS

Story (see *Before Class*)

BEFORE CLASS

Find a story approximately two pages in length. (Gattegno's *Short Passages* [Educational Solutions, New York City] contains ideal examples.) Pick out one or two long sentences that are of central importance in the story but do not occur at the beginning.

---

1 Tell students that you are going to read them a sentence (or two) but do *not* tell them where the sentences come from or why. Ask the students to write down as many words and phrases as they can remember. Warn them that you will read the sentence(s) only *once.*

2 Read the sentence and then ask students, working individually, to try to reconstruct it. If students appear to find the task too difficult, read the sentence a second time. Then have students continue their attempts at reconstruction. After they can make no further progress alone, suggest that they try working in pairs.

3 After a few minutes, tell students to change partners. Let them move freely around the room, comparing sentences. When the class is fairly near the "solution," but students are perhaps beginning to feel discouraged, tell them to sit down and put their books away.

4 Start reading the story that the sentence was taken from as if this were a completely new activity. The class will gradually realize that the sentence they worked on comes from the story. When you have finished, let students resume the reconstruction activity. Ask them to write the sentence on the board, working together as a group. With large classes you might need two parallel groups.

5 Finish by holding a discussion of the activity and the story with the whole class. What did they find most challenging? In the notetaking, were they distracted by trying to transcribe the material word for word? Or did they concentrate on picking out the main points? What *were* the main points?

Author
John Overton

Reading a Story to the Class 39

MATERIALS

Story (page 48)

BEFORE CLASS

Prepare the story by reading it quietly to yourself and then going through it several times aloud so that it will be "alive" when you present it to the class.

Level
Low intermediate and above

20–40

Language Functions
Narrating

Comparing

1 Teach any unknown vocabulary and set the mood for the story: quiet, calm, and comfortable.

2 Read the story (you will find the text on page 48). Use any pauses or simple dramatic gestures for effect. Make sure you look up from the book. Eye contact is vital. It will be far more difficult to hold the group's attention if you bury your head in the pages.

3 Since the story is unfinished, ask the students to form pairs or groups and write their own endings to it. Most students seem to want happy or trick endings such as: "The princess bribed the lionkeeper to feed the lion up so that it wasn't hungry," or "The King saw it as a sign from God when the lion turned away." Others may prefer a more twisted ending: "He fought the lion, won the fight, and then married the other woman anyway!" Circulate, helping the students express their ideas in writing.

4 When the groups have finished their versions, have a spokesperson from each group read their ending. Always start with the line ". . . acting on the decision she had made after days and nights of weighing the awful choice, she nodded to the right. The young man saw and without hesitating walked to the right-hand door and opened it." The class should share their feelings as a whole about each version.

5 Step 4 may lead to further discussion about *why* students wanted their particular end to the story; what kinds of stories they liked as children, or the fascination of ghost stories and fairy stories. Moreover, some students will probably have some stories they would like to tell or favorite characters they want to describe.

AUTHOR'S NOTE

This is an adaptation of a well-known story, "The Lady and the Tiger," by Frank R. Stockton. I first came across it in an examination set by the Ministry of Education of the United Republic of Tanzania.

Mo Strangeman

39 **Reading a Story to the Class** continued...

The Story

Many years ago in a country in North Africa there lived a king who had some very strange customs. One of these was the way he decided if a prisoner was guilty or not guilty. Whenever one of his subjects was accused of a serious crime, the king decided that the fate of the accused would be determined in front of the people. On the chosen day, the king, his followers, and all the people gathered on a small hill. In front of the hill was a big building with two doors, exactly alike, set side by side. At the king's signal, the accused would walk to the doors and open one of them. Behind one door was a hungry lion that would eat the prisoner as a punishment for his crime. Behind the other door was a beautiful woman to whom the prisoner would be married immediately as a reward for his innocence.

The plan seemed most fair to the king. The accused could choose his fate. He simply opened a door and was at once eaten or married.

Now it happened that the king's beautiful daughter, whom he loved above all things, had fallen in love with a poor but handsome young soldier. When the king found out that they loved each other, he put the young man into prison and set a day for his public trial. The king ordered the whole kingdom to be searched for the biggest lion and the most beautiful woman.

Finally, the day of the trial arrived. The young man entered the field. He was so handsome that the crowd greeted him with a hum of admiration and fear. How terrible this was for him! The handsome young soldier advanced into the field, turned, and as was his custom, bowed to the king. But he fixed his eyes on the princess, who was sitting on her father's right. The young man saw in her eyes that the princess knew on which side the lion was and on which side the lady. There was not a moment to lose. His eyes asked her, "Which door shall I choose?"

The princess knew that the woman her father had chosen was the loveliest in the land. In the past she had seen this woman throw admiring glances at the soldier. Sometimes she even suspected that these glances were returned. How could she bear to lose her love to another woman? How could she bear to see him torn apart by a lion? The princess paused. Then acting on the decision she had made after days and nights of weighing the awful choice, she nodded to the right. The young man saw and without hesitating walked to the right door and opened it . . .

Multiple Whispers 40

Level
Intermediate

Language Functions
Narrating

Expressing disagreement

MATERIALS	BEFORE CLASS
Stories (page 50)	Make one copy of the "Stories" page. Cut the individual stories apart.

1 Have the students sit in a circle and give each of them one of the short stories. Tell students to memorize the stories. Circulate, explaining vocabulary as necessary. Collect the stories so that you can use them again.

2 Ask every second student to turn to his or her *left-hand* neighbor and tell each other the stories they have memorized. If you have an odd number of students, join in yourself to make up an even number. After the students have finished, tell them to each turn to their *right-hand* neighbor and tell the story they have just been told (*not their original stories*). Students then exchange stories. Once again, they turn back to their (left-hand) neighbors and repeat the stories they have just been told by their other (right-hand) neighbors. The exercise can be continued either until all the stories have been passed around the group or the students start showing signs of boredom.

3 Ask each student to tell the group the last story he or she has heard. This is unlikely to bear much resemblance to the original, and students can become quite argumentative about exactly what was told to them. This final stage is a useful functional exercise for expressing disagreement. (The first stage is a good structural exercise for practicing the narrative past simple.) Finish by handing out copies of the stories so the class has a written record of the material.

Author
Randal Holme

Following are some sample stories. They are varied, and some of them are useful for promoting discussion about their meaning. Two have been intentionally selected because they are similar. Their use is particularly productive because the ensuing confusion produces genuine disagreement.

1 Once there was a head. The head saw so much that it wanted to be glass. The head saw everything. The head could not contain all it saw. The head burst into thousands of pieces. The pieces of glass became stars.

2 The king wanted to build a magnificent church. He found a builder. He said: "Build a church." The king was impatient. The builder finished the foundations and then he disappeared. The king was angry, but he could do nothing. After ten years the builder came back. The king wanted to kill him. The builder said, "The foundations are ready. Now I can finish the church."

3 The queen asked for a man to build an arch. She wanted an arch to pass through. A builder built the arch. When it was finished the queen passed under it. The arch was too low and knocked the queen's crown off her head. The queen said to the builder: "I will hang you." The builder said, "Hang the arch." When the queen hanged the arch, she raised it . . . .

4 The farmer liked to ride around his land on a donkey. Then he bought more land so he had to buy a horse. Then he bought more land so he had to buy a tractor. Soon he had so much land he had to buy a helicopter to go from end to end in one day. The helicopter was too fast. It took him over his land so quickly he thought the land was no longer his. He wanted to be large enough to eat all that his land produced. No man could be so large. He finally died of hunger.

5 The students asked their teacher: "What is the way?" The teacher did not answer. She only raised one finger. The next day, the teacher asked her students, "What is the way?" One student said, "The way is difficult," another said, "It is long," another said, "It is beautiful." "No, no!" the teacher said. She became angry. Then a student raised his finger. The teacher took a knife and cut the finger off. "That," she said, "is the way."

6 The Spanish fireman went to the fire. The fire was very dangerous. A woman was in the building. She could not leave. The Spanish fireman found a blanket. He called to the woman and said, "Jump into my blanket!" The woman was afraid. The fire grew more dangerous. The woman jumped. She fell towards the blanket. Just before she reached the blanket, the fireman waved the blanket away and shouted: "Olé!"

7 The Captain left England in 1786. He sailed into the Pacific. He went farther and farther south. He saw a ship without sails moving towards him. He sailed away. When he returned to England he did not recognize it.

8 A ship was sailing from London to New York. The captain saw another ship. He called to it. He heard no answer. He went close. He went onto the ship. He found everything on the ship in order. There was no sign of violence. He took the ship back to London.

9 There was a country where people did not make art like nature, but nature unlike art. One day an artist made a rock look like a head when before everyone had made rocks look unlike heads. The queen of the country was very pleased. She said: "the rock looks like me." A wise man said: "That head is better than your head! Now you must understand that as you are small and feeling small, you will act small; you will be like a beast."

10 A man bought a bottle. He opened the bottle and a genie flew out. The genie said: "What do you want?" The man wanted many things. The genie delivered them all. The man was surrounded by so many things that he could not climb over them. He was in prison.

Parallels 41

Level
Intermediate

40

Language Function
Sharing and summarizing
information

MATERIALS	BEFORE CLASS
Sentences (page 52)	Make a copy of the sentences for each group of eighteen students. Cut the sentences apart to form "sentence strips."

1 Deal the eighteen sentences out among the group. If you have fewer than eighteen students, it does not matter if some receive more than one strip. If you have a couple more than eighteen, let two students share one piece of information. Larger classes should be divided into two or even three groups.

2 Ask students to keep their strips secret. Their task is to memorize *the information* (not the actual sentences) on the strips. They should not learn the material "parrot fashion." Do not allow writing. Explain the vocabulary if necessary. Collect the strips so that you can use them again.

3 Ask students to mingle and share the information they have memorized. Give minimal instructions. Allow enough time for the information to be shared thoroughly but do not let it go on to the point where students become bored.

4 Ask students to return to their seats and write a summary of the information they have gathered. Students may work individually or in pairs.

5 When they have finished, students should compare their notes with other individuals or pairs. Next, working together as a group, students appoint a "secretary" and produce a final version on the board. At the end, if requested, you may give out copies of the original text for comparison.

Author
John Morgan

John F. Kennedy was murdered on a Friday.	Abraham Lincoln was murdered on a Friday
John F. Kennedy was shot in the head by Lee Harvey Oswald.	Abraham Lincoln was shot in the head by John Wilkes Booth.
Oswald shot Kennedy from a shop and then ran into a theater.	Booth shot Lincoln in a theater and then ran into a shop.
Lee Harvey Oswald was born in 1939.	John Wilkes Booth was born in 1839.
After the death of John F. Kennedy, Lyndon Johnson, the Vice-President, became President of the USA.	After the death of Abraham Lincoln, Andrew Johnson, the Vice-President, became President of the USA.
Lyndon Johnson was born in 1908.	Andrew Johnson was born in 1808.
John F. Kennedy had a secretary called Lincoln.	Abraham Lincoln had a secretary called Kennedy.
John F. Kennedy's wife was a brunette who spoke fluent French: she was 24 when she married Kennedy.	Abraham Lincoln's wife was a brunette who spoke fluent French: she was 24 when she married Lincoln.
John F. Kennedy's father, Joseph, was Ambassador to London.	Abraham Lincoln's son, Robert, was Ambassador to London.

42 Students for Sale

Level
Intermediate

30

Language Functions
Giving information

Persuading

MATERIALS	BEFORE CLASS
Magazines or newspapers	Cut out advertisements from magazines or newspapers, taking care to choose items that should appeal to your class. If you can't find any, think up a few imaginary advertising slogans and details of non-existent products and special offers.

1 Bring the materials you have gathered into class and use them to "brainstorm" advertising slogans. This will warm the group up in preparation for the second part of the activity.

2 Divide the class into pairs. One person in each pair is A, the other is B. Tell both the A's and the B's to think of a product they would each like to be. Once this has been decided, move into the marketing phase. A is the marketing person for B, and B is the marketing person for A. A must prepare a promotional advertising "spiel" for B, who meanwhile does the same for A. A and B should consult each other about what they should say. Exaggeration should be encouraged. Walk around the class, supplying vocabulary, helping with ideas if necessary, and correcting mistakes.

3 When the class is ready, each student presents his or her "product" to the group and gives the promotional spiel. The product should demonstrate some of the talents attributed to the corresponding student whenever possible. For example, the marketing person says she can speak French and the product says "Oui!" The promotion should be similar to a TV commercial, with a commentator and some visual action.

Author
Nancy Osmond

Creating Identities 43

MATERIALS	BEFORE CLASS
Index cards A large room with furniture that can be moved around easily	Write the key phrases on index cards as described in Step 4.

Level
Intermediate and above

60

Language Functions
Exchanging and comparing information

Narrating

1 Tell the class to divide themselves into three families or groups of people living together. Each family or group should make its own area, if possible using chairs, tables, boxes, and whatever else is available.

2 Ask the students to work out identities for themselves in their groups and to establish their relationships to one another. Ask them to build up their characters, referring to daily habits, deciding who financially supports whom, and so on. Stay in the background but provide help with vocabulary and structures as necessary. Try to let the identities come to the students themselves as much as possible.

3 Ask the three groups (who should remain in their areas) to face each other. Then tell them they should introduce themselves to the class.

4 Next, tell the groups to imagine that they all know each other. They should move around and establish among themselves when, where, and how they met. Introduce the past tense as required (see *Author's Note*). Use key phrases such as: "We met when we were in . . . ," "I first saw you . . . ," or "We went to . . ." written on cards that are passed to the students who need them.

5 Send the students "home" to their original areas and tell them it is, for example, early Friday evening and that they should act out what they would be doing in their assumed roles. Encourage them to move around, visiting each other's homes or going out.

6 After a few minutes shout out, for example, "It is now 10 PM. What are you doing now?" and then after a further few minutes, "It is now 1 AM," and so on. Continue in this way through Saturday and Sunday. In each case the characters should act out what they would be doing at the given time.

7 Finally, establish that it is Monday evening. Ask the students to gather around and face each other again. Use the material just generated to practice questions and answers in the past tense:
—Where did you go on Saturday night?
—I went to a concert.
—Did you meet Lucy?
—No, I didn't. I stayed at home.
—Why didn't you go out on Sunday afternoon?
—Because my mother came over for lunch.

AUTHOR'S NOTE

I use this activity primarily to *input* new structural material. However, such exercises can also be used as follow-up material for more advanced students. Moreover, this kind of exercise is neither limited to the past tense, nor to the concept of families. It could be adapted to the future, or set in a business context where the groups have to form corporations, agree about what they are trading, and then trade.

John Overton

 An Improvised Role-Play

Level
Intermediate

30

Language Function
Asking and
answering questions

MATERIALS	BEFORE CLASS
None	Requires no preparation!

1 Brainstorm on the board a concept or an object that will yield a rich collection of adjectives. For example, *the sea,* which might produce words such as *cool, calm, rough, unpredictable, blue, wet, stormy,* and *beautiful.* Other good words to start with are *space* and *garden.*

2 Ask the class which of the adjectives on the board could be applied to a person. Then ask the students to *imagine* an individual to whom all these words could apply and to spend a couple of minutes thinking about what sort of person he or she would be. Build up a quick, superficial outline of this character by asking questions like: "Is it a man or a woman? How old is he or she? What does he or she do for a living? What is his or her social background?" Do not dwell on the discussion at this stage; accept the first, spontaneous replies from the class.

3 Invite one student to assume the role of the character that has been suggested. Tell the others that this person is about to join them as a colleague at their place of work. Ask them to question this individual closely to

find out whether they will be happy to accept this character as a workmate. Is he or she the sort of person they think they could get along with? The role-player must develop the character but adhere as strictly as possible to the framework of the original adjectives applied to this particular individual. This will almost certainly involve their trying to work out any apparent contradictions in the group of adjectives.

4 When the students are confident they have an assessment of the role-player's personality, the others should each give a personal view of the character portrayed. The role-player should also join in the discussion on his or her character, retaining the role. Did the group correctly interpret the personality from the character's own point of view? This is a particularly rewarding exercise if you manage to finish by arriving at a consensus.

Author
Richard Baudains

The Open-Ended Interview **45**

MATERIALS	BEFORE CLASS
None	Select one or more characters from any story, dialogue, or book that the class has recently studied. It should be fictional (not a real-life person). Prepare questions to ask as described below.

Level
Low intermediate and above

5–20

Language Function
Asking and answering questions

1 Assign the role(s) of the character(s) to one (or more) of your higher-level students. Tell them to respond to the questions you ask them. Suppose the class has studied Poe's story "Cask of Amontillado." Announce that students X and Y are to be Montressor and Fortunato. Immediately begin by firing "nosey-reporter" questions at them (see *Author's Note*). These should be questions that do not have answers in the story. Simply invent the questions as you go along once you have used all your prepared questions.

2 Once the students are familiar with the game, let the class members themselves assume the roles of reporters interviewing the others. Finish with a discussion of how convincing the characters' accounts are. How would the other students have responded to the questions?

Example

Teacher: Fortunato, are you married?
Student X: Yes.
Teacher: What did your wife do when you failed to come home after visiting Montressor?
Student X: Well, you see, she was having an affair with him and she knew about the plot all along.
Teacher: Montressor, is that true?
Continue . . .

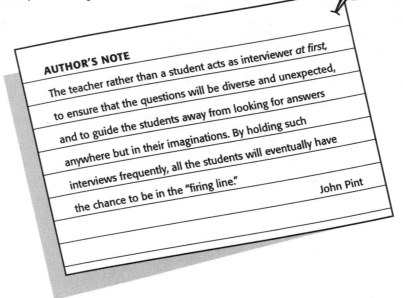

AUTHOR'S NOTE

The teacher rather than a student acts as interviewer *at first,* to ensure that the questions will be diverse and unexpected, and to guide the students away from looking for answers anywhere but in their imaginations. By holding such interviews frequently, all the students will eventually have the chance to be in the "firing line."

John Pint

46 Little Johnny's Accident

Level
Intermediate and above

60

Language Functions
Narrating

Justifying

Answering questions

MATERIALS	**BEFORE CLASS**
Overhead projector Figures (page 59)	Make an overhead projector transparency of the figures. Cut out the squares containing drawings of the characters, the stop sign, silhouette of the truck, etc.

1 Place the transparency piece showing the road on the projector. Move the cut-out of little Johnny riding his bicycle and tell the following story, laying the other cut-outs in the appropriate places at the appropriate times to illustrate the incident.

> "One day last week little Johnny was riding his bicycle along a narrow country lane. He wasn't paying attention because he was thinking about his dinner, so when he came to the stop sign he didn't stop. He went straight through. A truck was coming around the corner, and because the driver didn't see Johnny, he didn't stop. The truck hit Johnny. Ms. Brown was waiting at the bus stop on the corner and she saw the accident. Mr. Smith was driving his car in the other direction, and he saw the accident, too."

2 Ask the students to come to the front and move the cut-outs around and retell the story while the class corrects him or her on points of fact and grammar. (Do not spend more than about five minutes on this.)

3 This step involves setting up a role based on the accident. Assign the roles of Johnny, Ms. Brown, Mr. Smith and the truck driver; the remaining students play the parts of police officers. Depending on numbers, you may have to set up two parallel role-plays. Send each of the witnesses to a different part of the room and tell the police to go and interview them. Each officer should speak to at least two witnesses and they should take down written reports of the accident. Tell Johnny and Ms. Brown (privately) to insist that Johnny was not responsible. They should say, for example, that he did stop, the truck driver was drunk, Mr. Smith is nearsighted, and so on.

4 Bring the main characters and the police officers together in a courtroom scene. If you have had to work with more than one group you will need to set up two such scenes. The police officers make their reports and everybody tries to convince the judge (played either by the teacher or ideally by an outsider who knows nothing about the accident) that their version is correct. This usually involves a great deal of genuine disagreement because of the variety of different accounts. In this way the activity closely mirrors the problems that arise in everyday life when several witnesses to an incident all perceive it differently. You might like to round the lesson off with a discussion of this topic.

Author
Jim Brims

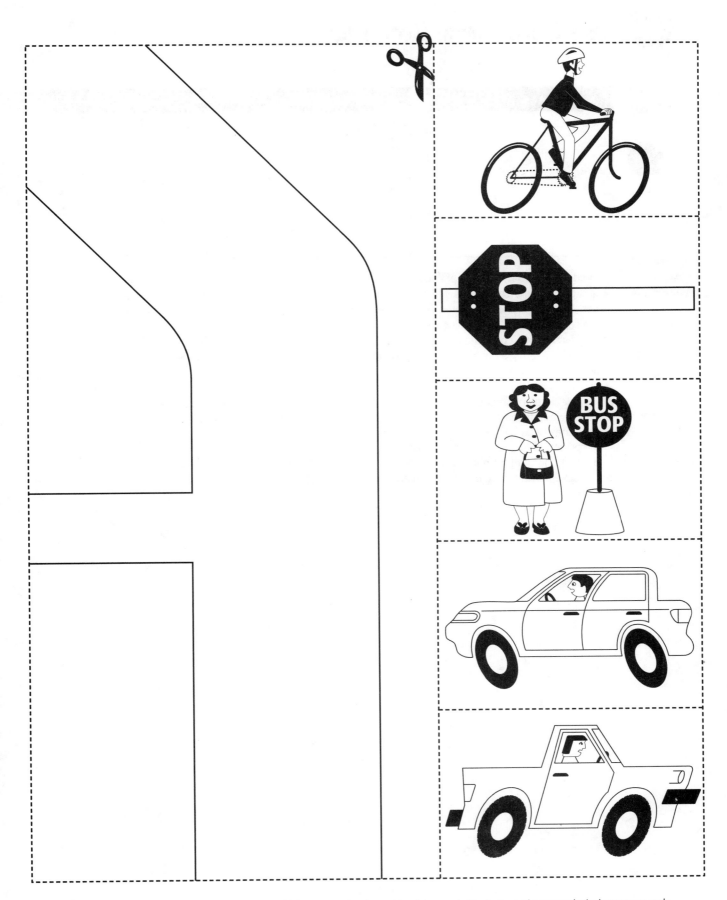

The Courtroom Role-Play

Level
Intermediate and above

Time
60–90
Depending on
inclusion of Step 3

Language Function
Making and
justifying decisions

MATERIALS

Court Cases (page 61)

BEFORE CLASS

Make enough copies of the court cases to distribute one different case per group and one list of judicial sentences per group.

1 Divide the class into groups of three or four. Give each group one of the court cases and a list of judicial sentences. Allow them fifteen minutes to reach a verdict and pass a sentence. Circulate, helping with vocabulary and points of information but *not* helping with ideas (for example, in Case 2, you might give details of how much an average family gets on welfare).

2 Where time and interest allow, you may wish to have each group try each case. When the groups have reached their decisions, each group should select a spokesperson to read out the verdicts. Write the verdicts on the board in chart form to allow for comparisons. List the possible penalties in the first column and then add

one column for each group's verdicts for each of the three cases. Finish off by inviting an open discussion of the various group verdicts.

3 The groups might then like to make up a case of their own, either suggesting a sentence, or offering it to another group to try, or both. Again, the verdicts should be written on the board as described in Step 2 and the lesson rounded off with a comparison of the verdicts and the groups' justifications.

Author
David Hill

Case 1

You Are the Jurors in a Criminal Court
A man, aged fifty, comes before you, accused of breaking into a hardware store and stealing woodworking tools worth $150. He pleads guilty.

You must reach a verdict and pass a sentence.

Points to consider:

1　He was a carpenter for thirty years with one company and was recently laid off.

2　He has been unemployed for six months.

3　He says that his only hope of finding work is to have his own set of tools.

4　It is his first offense.

Discuss this and come to a decision. What sentence would you pass? Why?

Case 2

You Are the Jurors in a Criminal Court
A woman comes before you accused of shoplifting at Sears. The police say she took two dishtowels and six glasses (total value $30). She pleads not guilty.

You must reach a verdict and pass a sentence.

Points to consider:

1　It is her first offense.

2　Her husband has been unemployed for one year.

3　She has six children.

4　She has lived in America for two years, but she can't speak English.

5　She says (through an interpreter) that she did not know that she had to pay, as the system is different in her country.

Discuss this and come to a decision. What sentence would you pass? Why?

Case 3

You Are the Jurors in a Criminal Court
A boy of fourteen comes before you accused of setting his school on fire. This caused $5,000 worth of damage. He pleads guilty.

You must reach a verdict and pass a sentence.

Points to consider:

1　He lives with his mother and four younger brothers and sisters.

2　His father died two years ago.

3　His mother works in a store during the day and in a bar in the evening to make enough money.

4　His grades are terrible and he is constantly in trouble for skipping class, fighting, and breaking rules.

5　It is not his first offense. A year ago he was accused of stealing $25 from the drugstore where he had a Saturday job. He was let go with a warning.

Discuss this and come to a decision. What sentence would you pass? Why?

Sentences

Possible Sentences for Cases 1, 2, and 3

Fine ($1,000 maximum)

Imprisonment (six months maximum)

Community service

Placement in a foster home
(persons under sixteen)

Placement in a reform school or similar facility
(persons under sixteen)

Probation

Acquittal

Recipes for Tired Teachers © 2004 Alta Book Center Publishers • www.altaesl.com
Permission granted to photocopy for one teacher's classroom use only.

48 Political Campaigns

Level
Intermediate

45–60

Language Function
Discussing and presenting
promises and intentions

MATERIALS	BEFORE CLASS
None	Requires no preparation!

1 Start a class discussion on the form of a typical election manifesto or platform statement and the language used in such statements. Build up a short list of examples on the board, similar to this:

My party is going to	increase public spending
We intend to	reintroduce the draft
Our plan is to	reduce taxation
We promise to	legalize drugs

2 Divide the class into groups of three or four (the optimal number being three groups total) and tell each group to decide on a political party. Encourage students to be innovative and imaginative—they need not follow established party lines. A few suggestions might be a drivers', cyclists', or pedestrians' party; a party for men's,

women's, or children's liberation; or a party dedicated to Latin American, European, or African unity.

3 Ask each group to prepare an election platform and to elect one member to present the party program to the rest of the class. Circulate, helping as necessary and correcting the language.

4 Have the party representatives make their speeches, one by one. Encourage questions and even heckling while they are speaking. Further questioning can take place once the speech is over, when any members of the party may be called upon to reply.

5 Finish with a mock election including a vote by secret ballot. Depending on the group, this could in turn provoke discussion of any recent political incidents or of a related topic such as comparative electoral systems or procedures, or even of the philosophy and principles underlying democracy.

Author
Sonia Taylor

Structures and Functions

49 **Introductions**

Level
Low intermediate
to intermediate

45

Language Functions
Introducing

Interrupting

MATERIALS	BEFORE CLASS
Labels or nametags	Requires no preparation!

1 Discuss different forms of etiquette and rituals of meeting people and compare them with the American forms. Who is introduced to whom? (Consider such variables as age, sex, status and so on. What do you say when you are introduced? Must you stand up?) Let the class initiate the forms of introduction as much as possible. Some basic examples might be:

- Could/Can/May I introduce you to . . .
- Let me introduce you to . . .
- Have you guys met before? Karl, this is Claudia.
- This is (my friend/my sister) Lisa.
- George—Agnes. (Agnes—George.)
- Sally, do you know/have you met . . .

Some examples of conversational gambits that may be used in maneuvering one guest away from another are:

- Can I interrupt/break in . . .
- Do you mind if I take her away/borrow her for a moment?
- Can you spare him for a moment?
- You (simply) must meet . . .
- There's someone I'm just dying for you to meet!

Consider any other examples you might want to use in reference to age, sex, social status, and environment. Encourage the students to draw on their own experience.

2 Divide the class into threes. Each student takes a turn at being the host or hostess and practices some of the language forms that have been looked at above.

3 Give the students labels or nametags. Ask each student to think of one well-known or imaginary person and one piece of information about this person. Students should then write the name and information on his or her label/nametag. Tell students to keep the information brief!

Examples:

4 Ask the students to attach the labels to their clothing. They can use their own character or swap the labels around in the group. They should then stand up and move around, introducing pairs of students to each other *in terms of these identities*, for example: "Captain Ashton, I wonder whether you have met Dr. Newton?" "Dr. Newton—Captain Ashton." Let the activity slowly develop into a kind of cocktail party, with the students introducing each other, circulating, interrupting, and building on the information provided.

Author
Chris Mills

Making Appointments 50

MATERIALS	BEFORE CLASS
Appointment Books (page 66)	Decide which version of the appointment books you want to use and make a copy of it for each student.

Level
Intermediate

 30

Language Functions
Making appointments

Socializing

1 Pre-teach or brainstorm the language required for making appointments and build up a list of expressions on the board. For example:

I have something I'd like to discuss with you.

When are you free?

I wonder if you could spare me a few minutes.

Could you make it on Monday? At 4 p.m.?

Yes/No, that would (not) be a convenient time.

2 Hand out a copy of the selected "Appointment Book" to each student. Ask students to complete the days or times on their page (first version: days; second version: times). Then ask students to fill in a number of the spaces with imaginary appointments, for example: budget meeting, yoga, dentist, English lesson, movie with friend. These appointments are fixed and cannot be changed. If pressed for time students should cross out a number of spaces. Not all the spaces should be filled in, however; for example, with ten students, at least nine spaces should be left blank on each student's page; with six students, at least five.

3 Ask students to make imaginary appointments with each one of their classmates. This means that in a class of ten, each student has to make nine appointments. (Divide large classes into groups of about ten.) You can also take part yourself. Try to speak to all the students so you can check their English. It is fairly easy to make the first appointments, but as the number of free spaces dwindles, the language has to become more complicated. In the end, students may be forced to agree that it is impossible to arrange some meetings as things stand. This could lead to the students' rearranging the dates already made.

Author
Derek Risley

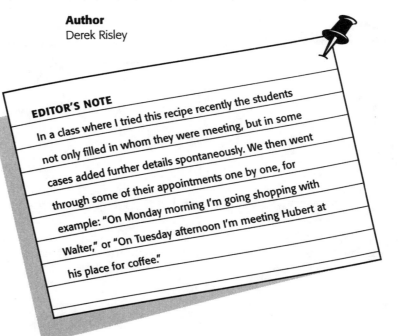

EDITOR'S NOTE

In a class where I tried this recipe recently the students not only filled in whom they were meeting, but in some cases added further details spontaneously. We then went through some of their appointments one by one, for example: "On Monday morning I'm going shopping with Walter," or "On Tuesday afternoon I'm meeting Hubert at his place for coffee."

Appointment Book 2

8:00–8:30	
8:30–9:00	
9:00–9:30	
9:30–10:00	
10:00–10:30	
10:30–11:00	
11:00–11:30	
11:30–12:00	
12:00–12:30	
12:30–1:00	
1:00–1:30	
1:30–2:00	
2:00–2:30	
2:30–3:00	
3:00–3:30	
3:30–4:00	
4:00–4:30	
4:30–5:00	

✂ -

Appointment Book 1

Day	Morning	Afternoon
	Weekend	

66

Telephone Conversation 51

Level
Intermediate

30

Language Functions
Socializing

Exchanging information

MATERIALS	BEFORE CLASS
None	Prepare a suitable telephone conversation that you can mime. It might be a good idea to use material from a textbook, although this activity works well with any telephone conversation as long as you can mime it clearly.

1 Present your mime to the class. Concentrate your efforts on *one* of the two speakers, getting responses from the students and writing the speaker's words on the board. Leave blank spaces for the second speaker's contribution. Allow time for practicing the intonation patterns and expressive voice tones. Try to introduce all the material by means of mime. For example, make the gesture of writing to indicate "Could you spell that, please?" or tap your wrist to elicit "What time?" You can also establish the situation of making a phone call by picking up an imaginary receiver and continuing as if keying in a number.

2 Go through the whole conversation from the beginning so that the class is thoroughly prepared both in what is written and in the missing half. Tell students to observe carefully, but do not let them write down any part of the conversation at this time. Now ask students to practice in pairs. One of the partners reads the written part while the other tries to fill in the second speaker's lines (those that are missing). Pairs who work quickly can change parts so that they both get a turn while the others finish.

3 Ask the class to provide the missing language and write it on the board in the spaces you have left. Accept any responses that make sense in the context even if they differ from your original script. You might also let students come to the front one by one and each write one of the responses. Once everything is correct, give the class the go-ahead to copy the material into their notebooks.

Author
William Atkinson

52 Making Requests

Level
Intermediate

20

Language Functions
Making requests

Adapting language
to social role

MATERIALS
Audio equipment
Recordings (see *Before Class*)
Cardboard or some type of flashcard paper

BEFORE CLASS
If you aren't able to find pre-recorded material, prepare audio recordings of common sounds that require a response of some kind, such as a kettle whistling, a baby crying, a telephone ringing, a car honking its horn, and a doorbell ringing. Also create flashcards illustrating different social roles and emotions. Use drawings or magazine pictures as illustrations. For example:

neutral social register	*formal social register*
babysitter	employer
secretary	banker
informal social register	*emotions*
brother or sister	anger
friend	love

1 Present the recorded sounds and ask students what they represent. Check effective recognition and teach any necessary vocabulary such as "the kettle's *whistling.*" Then present the flashcards and establish their significance by asking students to guess what sort of person or situation they represent. Don't worry too much if the students fall back on stereotypes at this stage. Make sure they appreciate the different language that would be used when talking to such a variety of people.

2 Play one sound effect and show one flashcard, for example, the phone ringing and the secretary. Ask for an appropriate (neutral) response such as "Would you answer the phone, please?" Then change the flashcard to the friend, for example, and say, "The phone's ringing" to show that this can also be used as a request to answer the telephone in an informal situation. Build up a table of responses on the board.

3 Show the flashcard symbolizing anger and say, "Answer the phone, will you?" using appropriate

intonation to show anger. Vary the combination of sound effects and flashcards to provide cues for further teacher-student practice, gradually developing into student-student practice. You might like to try adding to the initial responses so as to build up short dialogues such as:

(*Sound is a car honking its horn. Flashcard indicates friend or relative.*)
—Alistair's here. He's honking for you.
—Can you tell him I'll be down in ten minutes? I'm taking a bath.
—OK.

4 Round off the exercise with a discussion of cases in which *the situation* rather than someone's words requires us to say something. Examples might include a roof beginning to leak, change in the weather, knock at the door, malfunctioning machine, computer crashing, etc. What requests would be appropriate in these cases?

Author
Alan Cunningsworth

Interrupting 53

Level
Intermediate and above

15–30

Language Functions
Interrupting

Countering interruptions

MATERIALS	BEFORE CLASS
Interruptions (page 70) Short text to read aloud	Make a copy of the *Interruptions Worksheets* 1 and 2 for each student. Select a suitable text to read or prepare to speak on a subject for about five minutes.

1 Hand out a copy of Worksheet 1 to each student and work through it together. Explain the differences between the various interruptions. Which are formal and which are informal? Which could you use and which not use when speaking to a superior? How does intonation affect the formality of an interruption?

2 Tell the class you are going to read out a text or will talk for about five minutes and they should try to interrupt you *as much as possible,* using the phrases on the worksheet. The students can all interrupt together— the more expressions they call out the better. As you read or give your talk, counter the interruptions with replies such as those on Worksheet 2.

3 Distribute copies of Worksheet 2, one per student. Discuss the vocabulary and explain any new words and phrases. Divide the class into groups of four or five. Give the students a few minutes to prepare a talk or give them a passage to read aloud. Ask students in each group to read their passage or give their talks one by one while the others interrupt them as described in Steps 1 and 2. They should also counter the interruptions as outlined above. Allow each student about two minutes and then go straight to the next one, keeping the pace brisk.

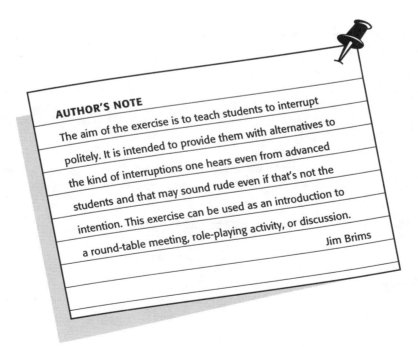

AUTHOR'S NOTE

The aim of the exercise is to teach students to interrupt politely. It is intended to provide them with alternatives to the kind of interruptions one hears even from advanced students and that may sound rude even if that's not the intention. This exercise can be used as an introduction to a round-table meeting, role-playing activity, or discussion.

Jim Brims

Interruptions Worksheet 1

Your teacher is going to start reading or speaking on a particular subject. You should try to interrupt him or her as often as you can. Put a check (✔) next to each phrase as you hear it. You should try to use each of the phrases at least once.

Phrases for interrupting:

I wonder if I could just interrupt you there . . .

Could I interrupt to say . . .

Do you mind if I say something here?

Sorry to butt in, but . . .

If I could just say something here . . .

I don't want to hold us up, but . . .

Asking for Clarification:

I wonder if I could ask for clarification on that point?

Could you be a little bit more specific?

I wonder if you could give us an example of that?

I'm afraid I didn't quite get that.

Expressing opposition or disagreement:

I'm afraid I don't agree with that . . .

Look, that really isn't quite right . . .

I don't see how it's possible to say that . . .

Yes, but on the other hand . . .

I really don't see how you can justify that.

Contradiction:

Yes, but if you say that the logical conclusion is . . .

You don't seriously think that, do you?

That can't possibly be right.

Annoyance:

Don't give me that!

That's nonsense!

Interruptions Worksheet 2

Now it is your turn to read or speak about a subject for two minutes. Don't worry about the content; just make sure you're talking. You will have to read or speak while the others interrupt you. Here are some useful phrases to counter the interruptions:

If you will allow me to continue . . .

I wonder if I could explain that point later . . .

If I could explain that at the end . . .

Just a moment, please, I won't be long.

I wonder if I could continue with what I'm saying . . .

I'll be glad to clarify any points at the end.

That's a very good question.

Let's try and stick to the point.

I've already dealt with that.

I'm coming to that in a moment.

Modal Drawings 54

MATERIALS	**BEFORE CLASS**
Picture sequences (page 72)	Enlarge, photocopy, and cut apart the picture sequences so that they can clearly be individually displayed at the front of the classroom. You may also wish to draw your own simple version of the sequences; in this case, practice doing so before class.

Level
Intermediate

30

Language Functions
Expressing possibility, impossibility, necessity, and disbelief

Making guesses and suppositions

1 Tell the class you want to practice modal verbs such as *may, might, must, could,* and *can't.* There are several ways in which the students can work. You can divide the students into pairs or small groups that later pool their ideas, or you can work with the class as a whole and control the lesson from the front.

2 Display or draw number 1 of the picture sequences on the board. Ask the class to use modals to comment on it. Accept statements such as "He's lying down" but encourage the students to concentrate on modals and to produce sentences like "He *might* have hurt himself" or "He *could* have fallen down." Refer to the list of captions on page 72. Collect as many sentences as you can.

3 Continue in the same way, adding further details step by step, as shown in pictures 2–5. (This procedure should be clarified by the sequence of pictures.) It is important to elicit the material *from the students.* Do not simply recite a stream of your own ideas, although you should prompt and encourage the class if they lack inspiration.

4 Finish the activity with one or both of the following suggestions:

A Have students tell the story, orally or in writing, either to a partner or the whole group. They should establish the causes of what happened.

B Have the groups produce new situations for which they produce their own drawings. Each group then elicits a story from the rest of the class.

Author
Ian Butcher

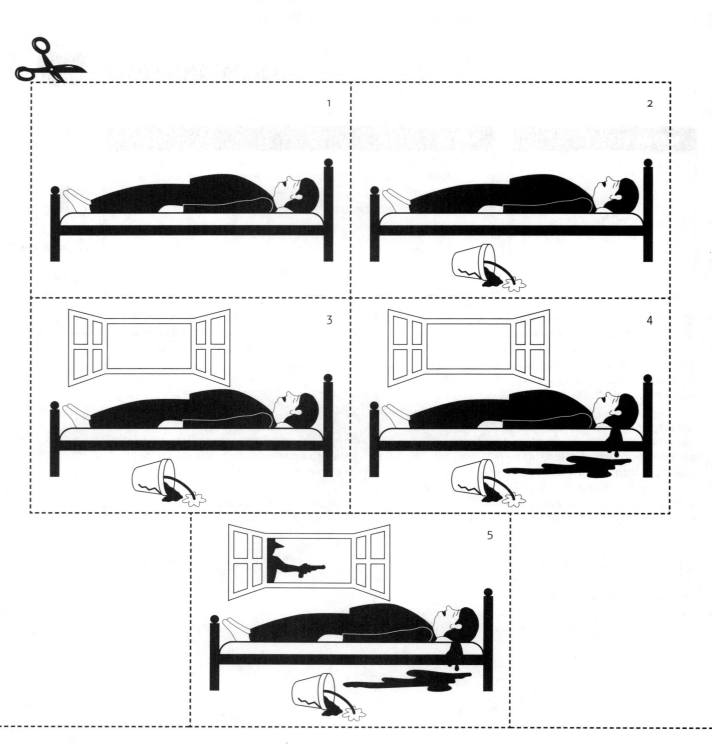

Picture 1

He might be sleeping.
He may even be dead.
He could just be resting.

Picture 2

He might be unconscious.
He must have been hit with the flowerpot.
He could be seeing stars.

Picture 3

The flowerpot must have fallen from the window.
The wind could have blown the window open.
Someone might have thrown the flowerpot at him.

Picture 4

He can't have been killed by the flowerpot.
He might have been shot.
It could just be a practical joke.

Picture 5

This man must have shot him.
He must have had a motive.
But he can't be dead! (with appropriate intonation)

The First and Second Conditionals

MATERIALS	BEFORE CLASS
None	Requires no preparation!

Level
Intermediate

Language Function
Expressing consequences
under given conditions

1 Discuss what your students habitually do and are likely to do again in the near future. You need to do this exercise with a class that has been working together for some time so that the students know each other well. Write five or six examples on the board, such as: "Brigitte always chews gum," "Jean stares out of the window," and "Heinz always asks lots of questions." Ask for more examples and add them on the board.

2 Ask the students how they will react if one of the people mentioned behaves as described, for example:

If Hilde speaks German in class tomorrow,
I'll scream.

If Bob chews gum with his mouth open again,
I'll move to another seat.

3 Change the names in the examples so that the habits are attributed to *other* students to whom they do not normally apply. This establishes a situation where the *second* conditional is required, for example:

If Ingrid spoke German in class tomorrow,
I would scream.

If Billy chewed gum with his mouth open,
I would move to another seat.

Pay particular attention to the stressed pronunciation of "would." Be sure to point out that in normal speech it would be contracted to "d."

4 Allow the exercise to open up naturally—you need *not* respond to the same behavior in the same way if it is displayed by different people, for example:

If Heinz doesn't stop asking me for answers,
I'll scream. But if Sonia kept asking me for the answers, I might ask her on a date.

If Renata tries to get another piece of paper from me, I'll tell her to get lost. But if Teresa tried to get a piece of paper from me, I'd give her the whole notebook.

Once again, be sure to practice the stress and intonation, which is particularly important in such contrastive examples.

Author
Mike Levy

56 Grammar Review

Level
Low intermediate
and above

10–20

Language Functions
Completing sentences

Asking questions

MATERIALS
None

BEFORE CLASS

Go through material already studied and make a selection of statements and questions students should be able to complete. Write them out clearly with the last part of each sentence left blank. For example:

- How can I . . .
- I can't . . .
- You have to understand . . .
- He should be . . .
- We were able to . . .
- She will tell you when to . . .

You can write these on the board or make a copy for each student.

1 Read the examples one by one, or hand out copies and ask the students to complete the sentences. Obviously, since the statements are all open-ended, there are numerous possible ways of completing them. Circulate, helping as necessary. When the students are ready, ask them to read their sentences aloud. Allow several students to complete an item before going on to the next one. For more advanced groups, encourage longer sentences. The exercises should be done *quickly* or it won't be much fun.

2 Another review exercise is to list the answers to a selection of questions in structures the students have studied. Students must then supply a question that would fit a given answer. In many cases there are several suitable possibilities as some answers, like those given below, clearly permit a wide range of questions. Again, this exercise should be done *rapidly*. Have all your cues written out beforehand so that you don't get confused and break the rhythm.

Author
Carlos Maetzu

EDITOR'S NOTE

Step 2 of this technique is described in greater detail in the following recipe, "Questions and Answers."

Answer	Possible Questions
No, I can't.	Can you swim/drive a car/say the alphabet backwards/stand on your head?
Mary	Who's that? What are you going to call the baby if it's a girl? What's your sister's name?
18	How old are you? How much is 9+9? How many cousins do you have?
I don't believe it!	Did you know I'm going to save up to buy a helicopter? Did I tell you I'm going to the moon on vacation?
Yes, you should.	Should I apply for that job? Should I come to your house tomorrow?

Questions and Answers

MATERIALS
None

BEFORE CLASS

Prepare a list of answers. The questions to these answers must allow the students to use certain forms of structures that they have already encountered. For example, "Right, then turn left at the traffic light," would be a suitable answer to the question, "How do you get to Fifth Avenue?" Unless you have decided to work on only one particular structure, try to prepare answers that test the whole range of question and verb forms covered thus far in class. See the examples in the table at the end of this activity.

Level
Intermediate

Language Function
Asking questions

Distribute the list of answers you have prepared as a handout or write it on the board. Students can work individually, in pairs, or in small groups. Their task is to prepare suitable questions for these answers. (See the examples in the table at the end of this activity.) If some students finish before others, tell them to think of further, alternative questions. Circulate, helping as necessary. Write the best answers on the board.

Variations

A   With more advanced classes this technique can also be employed to practice idiomatic phrases in the same way. Ask the students to provide suitable prompts for such expressions as: "Never mind," "Come off it," "You gotta be kidding!" or "No way!" Other good examples would be: "Certainly not!" "Serves you right!" "Sixty-five miles," "With two t's," and so on.

B   The students can also be asked to make a list of answers that are then distributed to other students to be "solved" as described in Step 1.

C   This variation is particularly well suited to "getting to know you sessions" at the beginning of a term or course. Ask the students to write down facts about themselves as short answers, for example: "21," "Blue," "Zagreb," "2004," "Twice," "Torquay and London," "Zlata," "Fishing and ballet," "Brad Pitt," "Steak and Cheese."

Divide the class into pairs. The partners must then make suggestions and try to establish the right questions to these answers. The answer "2004" might produce a conversation along the following lines:

A: Did you get married in 2004?
B: No, I didn't.
A: Perhaps you had a child?
B: No—not married, no children.
A: Was it at all connected with your family?
B: No. It was more to do with work.
A: You started work for the first time?
B: You're getting warmer . . .
A: Ah, I know! You graduated from college?
B: You got it!

Finally, armed with this information, each student tells the class something about the person he or she has been working with.

Author
Rick Haill

Answer	Possible Questions
I was held up by traffic.	Why were you late? Why didn't you arrive on time? Why didn't you call?
She burst into tears.	What happened when she realized she'd lost her passport? How did she react when she heard she'd won the scholarship?
Ever since I was a child.	Have you always been allergic to pollen? How long have you been learning the guitar?

Vocabulary (Lexis)

58 Crosswords

Level All	

Language Function
Making associations

MATERIALS

None

BEFORE CLASS

Select about thirty words that have naturally occurred in class and that you feel need review.

1 Write five of the words that need review on the board like the example in Figure 1. Then ask the class to make word associations diagonally, starting in the corners and working toward the center, so that each of the corner words eventually becomes linked up with the center word, as in Figure 2.

2 Give the students the list of words you have selected as needing review. Ask them to make *random* groups of five words from the selection and

to write them down, as in Figure 1, that is with one in the middle and one in each corner. They should not begin by choosing five connected words. Then ask them to write their individual associations, as done in Figure 2.

3 After ten to fifteen minutes ask the class to compare their ideas and associations in pairs or small groups.

Author
Mike Lavery

Figure 1

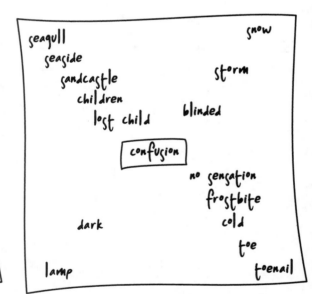

Figure 2

Vocabulary Review 59

MATERIALS	BEFORE CLASS
Small cards, preferably in sets of different colors	Prepare two *different* sets of twenty to thirty words written on cards (one word per card). It is a good idea to use a different color for each set of cards in order to distinguish them easily. The words chosen should be mostly nouns that have occurred in previous lessons and now require review.

Level
Intermediate

30

Language Function
Making associations

1 Divide the class into two groups and give each half one of the sets of cards. Let the groups read their words aloud and then determine the meanings *among themselves.* Neither group should know the words the other group has received.

2 Have each group choose six of their words (one word for each student—see *Author's Note* below) that they feel have related meanings. At first, the themes of the associations are not obvious, but when the activity is repeated the students usually try to find more imaginative connections.

3 Ask each student to write his or her word in a sentence. Thus each group will have six sentences. Again it should *not* be obvious which word each sentence is formed around—see Step 4. Tell the groups to exchange their sentences orally in pairs, with each student from Group 1 working with a partner from Group 2.

4 Ask students to re-form their original groups. Each student is to report back with the sentence he or she has heard from the other group. It is a good idea for a group secretary to write the sentences down. Tell the students to look carefully at the six sentences and to try to find which words and associations the other group had chosen and the themes of association.

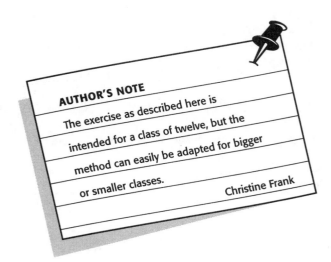

AUTHOR'S NOTE

The exercise as described here is intended for a class of twelve, but the method can easily be adapted for bigger or smaller classes.

Christine Frank

60 Confused Words

Level
Intermediate and above

50–60

Language Function
Identifying and contrasting vocabulary

BEFORE CLASS

Make a list of words that are commonly confused by students at the level you are teaching. Make sure you are able to give a clear explanation of the difference between the words; some of them are trickier than they appear. A sample of suggested words is listed below. Get a slip of paper for each student. On each slip, write three of the words from the list. The three words should all be from different "confused" pairs. It may be necessary to duplicate some items, depending on the number of students in your class. If there are more words than three per slip of paper, make sure that you use both words in each pair, meaning the leftover words will still be paired up (see Step 1).

1 Distribute one "mini list" of three words to each student. Explain that they must circulate and try to find the words from the other students' pieces of paper that are commonly confused with the ones they have on their own pieces of paper. Gino, for example, might have AFFECT/INDUSTRIAL/OCCASION. His job is to find the three classmates who have EFFECT, INDUSTRIOUS, and OPPORTUNITY. (This is why the words each student is looking for should be distributed among three different students on three different pieces of paper.) You should circulate around the room, advising, listening, and answering questions.

2 To introduce a competitive element, you may wish to stop when the first student has completed the task. Otherwise, continue until everyone has finished. Give those who are ready another example or two to keep them busy, but make sure you leave adequate time for illustration and explanation of all the words.

3 Ask students to write a couple of sentences to bring out the different meanings of the words they have successfully matched. Go around the group and check what they have written. Finally, ask students to read their words and sentences aloud and invite comment from the others. You may find that this activity prompts students to talk about other lexical points they find confusing.

Sample List of Confused Words

rob/steal	presently/actually
passed/past	prevent/avoid
loose/lose	economic/economical
say/tell	principal/principle
adopt/adapt	human/humane
price/prize	error/fault
moral/morale	affect/effect
rise/raise	industrious/industrial
sensible/sensitive	opportunity/occasion

Author
Rick Haill

The Cut-Out Bedroom 61

Level
Intermediate

45–60

Language Functions
Expressing spatial
relationships

Describing

MATERIALS

Construction paper
in various colors

Felt pens

Scissors

BEFORE CLASS

Assemble a set of materials for every group of three to four students. Each set should consist of a large piece of construction paper with a large rectangle drawn on it, several smaller pieces of contrasting-color paper, a cutout of a rug and bed, felt pens, and scissors.

1 Divide the class into groups of three or four, and give each group one of the sets of materials. Tell the students to do what they wish with the materials. (You may want simply to distribute the materials, say nothing about them, and leave the room briefly, letting the class decide what they are going to do with them.) After a discussion, students generally come up with the idea of planning a bedroom, although some groups may prefer to plan a different room or even a whole house.

2 If the students do not start planning a room (or house), suggest that they do so. While the students are discussing their plans (and making cutouts for other furniture) they will be thinking spatially and using spatial

prepositions (for example, near, beside, in front of, behind). They will also be making group decisions about what is needed and where it is to be put. During this time, circulate around the room and elicit appropriate language such as "near wall," "far wall," and "top right-hand corner." Point out or elicit the relative nature of these expressions—they differ depending on where the speaker and listener are located. For example the "near wall" to one person is the "far wall" to a person sitting opposite him or her.

3 When the groups have completed their plans, encourage them to look at other groups' efforts and discuss them with their creators.

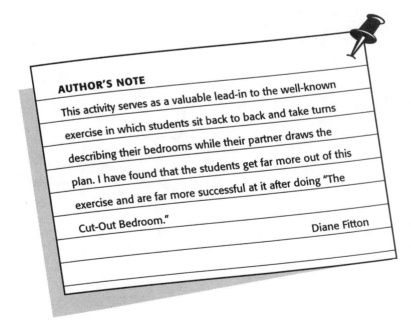

AUTHOR'S NOTE

This activity serves as a valuable lead-in to the well-known exercise in which students sit back to back and take turns describing their bedrooms while their partner draws the plan. I have found that the students get far more out of this exercise and are far more successful at it after doing "The Cut-Out Bedroom."

Diane Fitton

 **Practicing Phrasal Verbs**

Level
Intermediate and above

Language Function
Practicing phrasal verbs

MATERIALS
None

BEFORE CLASS
Requires no preparation!

1 Ask each student to bring between one and four sentences that contain phrasal verbs to the next class. They should be clear about the meanings and should be prepared to explain them. Typical examples would be: "Please *pick* me *up* at 8:00 tomorrow," "I'll *take* you *on* at chess anytime," "The meeting *broke up* earlier than expected."

2 At the next class, divide the students into groups of about three or four. Ask the students to teach each other their verbs. Quickly go around checking that the verbs are used correctly, explaining as necessary and answering any questions.

3 When the groups are clear about the meanings, ask them to make up stories including as many of their phrasal verbs as possible. Tell them that each group should be ready to mime its story to the rest of the class. Circulate, again helping as necessary and discreetly

supervising the rehearsal of the miming once the stories have been written.

4 Ask one group to act out its story in mime. The others have to try to establish which phrasal verbs are being depicted. Then have the group repeat its mime. This time, the audience can "freeze" the actors, ask them questions (which they can answer verbally), and if possible, write the verbs on the board as they come up.

5 If time and interest permit, let each group perform while the others try to spot the phrasal verbs in the same way. Make a note of all the verbs to practice later. (Start by checking that they know them at the next lesson.)

Author
Katya Benjamin

PUBLISHER'S NOTE

Lists of phrasal verbs can easily be found online at Dave's ESL Café, www.eslcafe.com. The direct link is http://www.eslcafe.com/pv/.

Signs **63**

MATERIALS	BEFORE CLASS
None	Requires no preparation!

Level
Low intermediate
to intermediate

Language Function
Interpreting signs

1 Brainstorm signs, for example: *Keep Left, Keep Off the Grass, Wet Paint, No Trespassing,* and *No Vacancies.* Write the material on the board. Ask the class what they think the signs mean and where they might be found. Explain as necessary. For example, "No Vacancies" would probably be seen in front of a motel or inn and means that it is full.

2 Divide the class into pairs or groups of three and tell them to prepare a mime or short skit to illustrate one of the signs. For instance, to illustrate "No Vacancies," a student might play the part of a tourist looking for a room with another as a hotel manager or clerk.

3 Have each group perform its skit. The actors should not specify what sign is being represented, as guessing is the task for the rest of the class.

4 As a follow-up, you may want to have students go out and note two or three new signs for discussion at the next class. If you are teaching in a country where there are no English signs, tell the students to collect the signs in whatever languages they can. Their task at the next class will be to translate them into English.

5 Another productive idea is to ask the students to think up new signs for anything they might like to stop, promote, or draw people's attention to. They should explain why they feel these signs are necessary so that the activity can be rounded off with a lively discussion. The signs could be written on pieces of paper and put on the classroom walls.

Author
Richard Baudains

64 Vocabulary Expansion

Level
Intermediate

45

Language Function
Categorizing vocabulary

MATERIALS	BEFORE CLASS
Large sheets of paper Felt-tip pens	Requires no preparation!

1 Ask for two student volunteers, one who likes drawing and one with clear handwriting. Get the artist to start drawing a courtroom and the people in it. As he or she draws on the board, the other student, the "secretary," should write in the names of the parts of the room such as "bench" and "witness stand" and the descriptions of the people, for instance, "judge" and "defense attorney." When the secretary does not know a word, he or she should ask the class, or as a last resort, the teacher.

2 Distribute the sheets of paper and felt-tip pens. Ask the students to copy the board drawing, writing in the nouns needed to designate the objects and people in the appropriate places. This is to consolidate the vocabulary that has been introduced in Step 1.

3 Tell the students you are going out for five minutes. When you come back you want them to have organized themselves into a courtroom, with different students taking different roles and standing or sitting in the appropriate parts of the room. When you come back into the room, go up to the students and ask them questions

such as: "Where are you?" "Who are you?" "Who do you like in this room?" or "Who do you sympathize with?" This activates the vocabulary generated and sets it in an affective frame by making the students take on the parts of the defendant, witnesses, jury, and so on. It is important to note, however, that this activity is not intended as a straightforward role-playing exercise.

4 Tell the students to return to their seats and to organize the courtroom vocabulary they know into categories. The only rule is that they must *put each word into at least two categories*. (For example, "witness stand" could go into a category of "furniture" and one of "connected with the defendant.") It is important *not* to give examples of what you mean by categories—let the students work it out for themselves. When they have organized the words into their own categories, get the students to read out their lists. This gives you a final check on pronunciation and stress. Allow students to ask for an explanation of each other's classification but be sure they respect each other's personal associations.

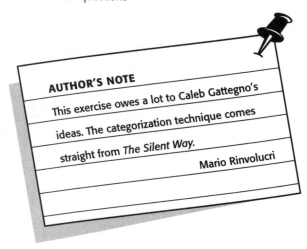

AUTHOR'S NOTE

This exercise owes a lot to Caleb Gattegno's ideas. The categorization technique comes straight from *The Silent Way*.

Mario Rinvolucri

Vers in Motion  65

Level
Intermediate and above

Language Function
Describing movement

MATERIALS	BEFORE CLASS
Illustrations (see *Before Class*)	Prepare a list of verbs of motion geared to the level of your class together with suitable situational prompts (cues) or illustrations to accompany them. Make a copy of the list for each student. Plan the material to be spread over several sessions depending on the group. (Remember that it has been estimated that the average student can absorb a maximum of only seven new words of expression in any one lesson.)

1 Let the class choose a name, say "Pat," to provide a focal character for the basic sentence, which should be written on the board like this:

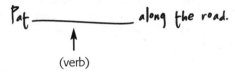

Pat ————————— along the road.
↑
(verb)

Begin by giving a simple example such as "Pat is exercising." Here a suitable verb is "jog," so that the model becomes:

Pat jogged along the road.

Or, if Pat was not very healthy, the model might be:

Pat huffed/trudged/stumbled along the road.

There is a list of fifty suggested prompts (cues) and verbs at the end of this recipe.

2 Act out or illustrate the verbs as you give the prompts, and explain them as necessary. Except with very advanced classes, it is advisable to give the students a list of the verbs you have chosen. This may be done in advance, so that they can mull over them. It should ensure that students will produce more verbs and that they can contribute more to the discussion of similarities and differences among the verbs. To round off each session, reverse the procedure: give students the verbs and ask them to recall the prompts or situations. For example:

Pat jogged along the road. She was exercising.

Pat trudged along the road. She was tired.

3 As a follow-up, either choose students who enjoy drama and get them to act out some of the verbs from your list, or mime the action yourself. In either case, have the students guess the verbs. Groups can also be asked to work out a short mime story that they then present to the class. The other students are then asked to describe the action, using the new vocabulary wherever possible.

Author
Rick Haill

Suggested List of Prompts and Verbs

Pat was . . .
in a car = drove
in a very fast car = sped/raced
in an old car = squeaked/rattled
in an old car on a bad road = bumped/jolted
on a bicycle = cycled/pedaled
an old man on an old bike = wobbled
on a fast motorcycle = sped/zoomed/hurtled
on a pony = trotted
riding a horse quite quickly = cantered
on a race horse = galloped
a soldier = marched/paraded
a policeman = patrolled/proceeded
in no hurry = ambled/strolled/sauntered
lame = hobbled/limped
very tired = plodded/trudged
very old = shuffled
a baby = toddled/crawled
very proud and self-important = swaggered/strutted
a happy child = hopped/skipped
trying to keep fit = jogged
in training for the hundred meters = sprinted/sped
leading a cavalry attack = charged
a burglar = stole/prowled/crept
a ballet dancer = leapt/pirouetted
in a good mood = breezed/cavorted/frolicked
in a bad mood = stomped/stamped
an acrobat = cart-wheeled/somersaulted
in a Rolls Royce = glided

driving a tank or a bulldozer = rumbled
in a steam engine = chugged
The road was icy = She slipped/slid
The road was deep in snow = She trudged/skied/slogged
The road was two feet deep in water = She waded
It was pitch dark and/or a thick fog = She groped/felt her way
She didn't want to disturb anyone = She tiptoed

And some less serious ones . . .
Pat was . . .
a slob = drooled
a fox = slunk/sneaked
a snake = slithered
a butterfly = fluttered
wearing very high heels = teetered/wobbled
David Beckham (or any famous soccer player) = dribbled
Michelle Kwan (or any famous figure skater) = skated/glided/twirled
Michael Jackson = shimmied/rocked/gyrated/moon-walked
lost or a poet = wandered/meandered
a student trying to hitch a ride = hitchhiked/hitched/thumbed
overweight or a duck = waddled
into levitation = floated
acting suspiciously = sidled
on an airplane = jetted, streaked

66 More About Verbs in Motion

Level
Intermediate and above

Language Function
Describing movement

MATERIALS
Index cards

BEFORE CLASS
Prepare cards with verbs written on them—see Step 5. Make sure you can mime or explain any words that might come up.

1 Draw a diagram showing two locations, for example, a house and a supermarket, or simply A and B, on the board. Tell the class you want to look at some of the different ways we can go from one place to another, for example "run" or "stagger." You can find some more examples in List A at the end of this recipe. Pick out a suitable selection for your group.

2 Ask the students to come up in groups of two and three and write as many verbs of motion as they can think of on the board. If they do not know the exact word they want they should either draw the action or write a clue, for instance, "on one leg" instead of "hop." Prompt as necessary with examples such as "The sidewalk was icy," or "What if you're tired?" or "Say you're on a bicycle," and so on.

3 Discuss the words and their applications. Decide on clues as to the meanings and write or draw them on the board beside the relevant words, for example: "rush" = "he was in a hurry" or ⚡⚡⚡ = "crawl." Then erase either of the clues, leaving only the verbs, or the verbs leaving only the clues. Go through them with the class.

> **AUTHOR'S NOTE**
> This approach to teaching verbs of motion developed from using the ideas described in my husband's recipe "Verbs in Motion" (see page 85).
> Allison Haill

4 As an initial follow-up, divide the class into two teams, each of which has to make a list of ten to twelve verbs from those covered in the lesson. A member of team A must then mime a word given him or her by team B *to his or her own team,* who have to guess it. Team B may choose to give either the verb itself or the clue as the answer. Then the other team has a turn and so on.

5 Several lessons later, follow up by dividing the class into two teams or groups. Give each group a card with a selection of items from the suggestions in List B. (You can find even more examples in the recipe "Verbs in Motion" on page 85.) The cards should be different, and one or two new verbs may be included. Separate the groups, sending one group out of the room if possible. Quickly check that the students know all the verbs on their cards and that they can mime them. Then have each group take turns at miming its verbs for the other students to guess. The comic aspect of this activity helps impress the words on the students' memories.

List A—Suggested Verbs for Part 1 (Steps 1–4)

amble	hop	plod	slide	trudge
bump	hurtle	race	slip	wade
crawl	jog	ride	sprint	wander
creep	jolt	sail	stagger	weave
gallop	limp	shuffle	stroll	zigzag
hobble	pedal	skip	tiptoe	zoom

(Naturally you do not have to teach *all* these verbs, particularly if your class knows hardly any of them.)

List B—Suggestions for Part 2 (Step 5)

He or she was . . .
- training for the 100 meters = sprinted
- depressed and tired = trudged
- lame = limped
- in a hurry = ran
- not in a hurry = strolled
- on a bike for the first time = wobbled
- wounded in the stomach and unable to get to his or her feet = dragged himself or herself
- on a road two feet deep in water = waded
- full of himself or herself = sauntered
- on a racehorse = galloped
- on a motorbike = zoomed
- a burglar moving stealthily = crept

Fun and Games

67 **Picture Dialogue Game**

Level
Low intermediate
to intermediate

20

Language Function
Writing dialogues

MATERIALS	BEFORE CLASS
Magazines and/or other sources of pictures	Collect six to ten pictures of two people talking to each other.

1 Display the pictures at the front of the class. Make sure that all students can see them clearly.

2 Arrange students in pairs and ask each pair to choose one of the pictures to use as the basis of a short dialogue. Each pair should not know the pictures that other pairs have chosen. Give each pair three or four minutes to write down what they think the two people in their picture are saying. Circulate, checking that the language is correct and helping as necessary.

3 Ask the pairs to read or, better still, act out their dialogues, each partner taking one role while the rest of the class tries to guess which picture has been chosen. Whenever possible, the students should justify their guesses.

Author
Christine Frank

Picture Question Game

Level
Low intermediate
to intermediate

Language Function
Asking and
answering questions

MATERIALS	BEFORE CLASS
Magazines	Cut out three fairly detailed pictures from magazines. Street scenes or household interiors that contain a lot of detail are most suitable.

1 Hold up one of the pictures to the class for about forty-five to sixty seconds. Then put the picture down where no one can see it and ask memory questions such as: "What color is the . . . ?", "How many . . . are there?", "What's on the right of the . . . ?", and so on. Tailor your questions to the needs and level of your class. You may wish to show the picture two or even three times, following each showing with further questions as described above.

2 Divide the class into two teams, A and B. Give each team one picture. Tell them to prepare twelve memory questions for the other team to answer. Go around and check that the questions are in correct English.

3 Team A is shown Team B's picture for up to a minute. Team B now asks its questions, which Team A has to answer. Award points for correct answers. Write the points on the board or appoint a student "secretary." The questioning can take place in several ways:

  A Team B members can take turns asking the questions with Team A members either answering in turn or working together as a panel.

  B You may also pair students from the teams so that each student works with a partner from the opposing team. This maximizes student participation, since *each* student asks, or has to answer, *all twelve questions.* If the class works this way, it is of course essential for each team member to have all the questions in written form.

  C Each member of Team B takes two or three questions and asks them of Team A, one by one. After the questioning, however it is done, Team A should be allowed to see the picture again to check both the points its members had not remembered and those that they had.

4 Now show Team A's picture to Team B. Repeat Step 3 with Team A as inquisitors and Team B as respondents.

Author
Saxon Menné

Picture Game

Level
All

Language Functions
Describing

Asking questions

Evaluating content

MATERIALS	BEFORE CLASS
Magazines	Find one or two interesting magazine pictures. Mount them on cardboard.

1 Explain the activity clearly to the class. Tell them you are going to give a picture to one pair of students so that only they can see it. Both members of the pair will then offer what is claimed to be a description of the picture, but only *one* description will be accurate. The other account will be invented. After each of the two students has offered his or her description, the rest of the class should ask questions to try and determine which account is true and which is false.

2 Select the pair of students and give them a picture. If it isn't mounted, you may need a piece of cardboard to hold behind it to ensure that it remains secret—the class should not be able to see through it if it is held up to the light.

3 Ask the two students to decide quietly who will invent and who will tell the truth. Then have them prepare their description. (This might be assigned as homework so they will have enough time to prepare their accounts in more detail.)

4 The two chosen students present their descriptions to the class. Should the pace lag when the questions are being asked, or should the class be certain that they have found out the truth, stop and ask why they think as they do. Discourage answers like, "Well, I just think so." The students should try to give reasons for their opinions.

5 Show the class the picture, and discuss its content. If interest is high, you may wish to select another pair and repeat the exercise with a different picture.

Author
Randal Holme

Guess the Object 70

Level
Intermediate

20

Language Function
Describing

MATERIALS

Slips of paper

BEFORE CLASS

Write names of objects on slips of paper. For example: *cell phone, lipstick, television set,* and *pair of binoculars.* Fold the slips in two so that the writing cannot be seen. The vocabulary should be restricted to objects that the students know and can identify in English.

1 Teach or review spatial relationships between objects and lines and various related vocabulary. Expressions that the students will need to use might include: *above, below, at right angles, parallel, on the left/right, higher, lower, further up/down/left/right, round, square, rectangular, triangular,* etc.

2 Ask a student who can draw to go to the board. Ask another student, or perhaps a pair of students, to take one of the slips of paper at random. This student's (or pair's) task is to describe the object written on the slip, *without saying anything about its function.* In other words, a ruler should be described as "having a series of regular marks along its side" and *not* as "an object for measuring things." A television set is described as "one rectangle (the screen) within a larger rectangle (the cabinet) with some small circles (the controls) at the bottom."

3 The "artists" must try to draw what is described while the rest of the class use this drawing together with the oral description to guess the object. The student(s) dictating the description should correct the artist by giving further instructions, for example, "No, the second rectangle is smaller," or "Put it a little further to the left."

4 The student who first guesses the object correctly picks another slip at random and the activity continues. You may wish to have this student choose a partner to work with. This activity is far more demanding than it sounds if students strictly adhere to the rule about not saying anything regarding the objects' functions.

Author
Miranda Britt

71 Find the Owner

Level
All

20

Language Functions
Making guesses and suppositions

Expressing (im)possibility and necessity

MATERIALS	BEFORE CLASS
Large bag or box	Requires no preparation!

1 Tell students to each choose an object that they have with them, but not to let anyone else see it. Go around the room collecting the objects in a suitable container, not forgetting to put in something of your own. If you have a very small class, say six students or fewer, you may wish to ask for two objects from each participant.

2 Either empty the contents of the container onto the table or take the objects out one by one. Be careful—some people may have put in something fragile such as a watch. Make it clear that the students should *not* say which objects are theirs at this stage.

3 Work through the objects individually, asking the class to name or describe each one, and build up a list on the board. Elicit vocabulary from the class. Encourage students to describe the objects as well as name them.

4 Tell the class that their next step is to establish which objects belong to which people. Take them one by one. With beginning or low-intermediate groups, use formulas such as: "This is _____'s" or "I think this is _____'s." The students should give reasons wherever possible. This can be done quite simply:

> Peter: I think the hairclip is Angela's.
> Angela: But my hair is too short for a hairclip.
> Rosa: I think it's Courtney's. She has long hair.

> Courtney: I don't wear hairclips. I think it's Barbara's because she is the only other person in this group who has long hair.

In this short example Barbara can now admit that it's hers. Make sure there is always a lot of discussion and speculation before the students claim their objects.

With higher-level groups, use combinations of the following structures:

> "It may/might/could/must/can't/couldn't be _____'s (because) . . ."

For example:

> Christine: It looks like a man's watch, but as some women wear larger watches these days, it *could* belong to a woman.
> Frank: Yes, but all of us are wearing watches now except Richard, so it *must* be his.

The activity finishes when all the objects have been claimed.

Authors
Saxon Menné
Christine Frank

If I Were You . . .

MATERIALS	BEFORE CLASS
None	Requires no preparation!

Level
Intermediate

20

Language Functions
Speculating

Expressing consequences

1 In this game one member of the group is sent out of the classroom while the others decide on a profession that person is to assume. When the person comes back, the others must make subtle remarks using the structure "If I were you . . ." For example, if it has been decided that the person is a boxer, the students might say:

"If I were you I'd jump rope everyday."
"If I were you I'd give up smoking."

2 A few of these examples should be prepared while the person is still outside. Don't let the class choose a profession for which nobody can think of anything to say! It is also important to avoid obvious examples such as: "If I were you I'd serve meals in a restaurant everyday."

3 Call back the person who was sent out. This student's task now is to find out what his or her assumed profession is. The person can ask the others questions using "If you were me would you . . . ?" to try to establish the designated profession. Some examples might be: "If you were me, would you work outdoors or indoors?" "Would you make a lot of money?" "Would you have to be able to type?" (It is a good idea to tell the one who is "it" to prepare a few appropriate questions while he or she is out. This provides something for the person to do while waiting and should help to keep things moving while the game is going on.)

4 If the group gets stuck, try helping by slipping them pieces of paper with ideas on them, say "gloves," "lose weight," or "look fit" for the boxer. You can also send the person out again and re-prime the group if things have reached a standstill. Another possibility if the class loses ideas is to make the one who is "it" turn his or her back while you mime relevant cues such as a waiter carrying a tray, writing down an order, or taking a fly out of somebody's soup!

Author
Ian Butcher

93

Grammar Game

Level
Low intermediate
and above

20

Language Function
Appreciating grammar

MATERIALS	BEFORE CLASS
None	Requires no preparation!

1 Ask the class to write any grammar points they are not sure of on pieces of paper, which you should then collect. Typical examples might be "the conditional" or "used to." Go through the points, either quickly during the class or as preparation for a later lesson if you feel unsure of your knowledge of English grammar. Then select *one* point that you can explain clearly and that you feel can be used productively in the way described below.

2 Ask one student to leave the room with the task of preparing as many questions as possible about anything. There should be no restrictions concerning the subject matter. Meanwhile, go over the grammar point you have selected with the rest of the group. Whenever possible let those students who understand the point explain it to the others.

3 Bring the student back in, and have him or her ask the questions. The others reply *using the tense or*

grammar point that is being practiced in as natural a sentence as they can. For instance, if you were doing the conditional and the question was "What are you doing tomorrow?" the answer might be: "I'll be sitting here working as usual, but if I'd taken that other job I was offered I'd probably have gone on vacation." The next question might be: "What do you think about nuclear power?" to which suitable replies would be: "I'd have been much happier if it had been prohibited years ago" or "If it hadn't been for the accident at Three Mile Island, I think I'd probably be in favor of it." The replies may be true or imaginary. The questioner has to guess which structure has been chosen. The object of the game is to think of a variety of contexts for the use of the point being practiced.

Author
Marjorie Baudains

Grammatical Snakes and Ladders 74

Level
All

35

Language Function
Asking questions

MATERIALS

Playing board (page 96)

A die

Rules (page 97)

Playing pieces (i.e., coins), one for each student

BEFORE CLASS

Make copies of the playing board and rules for each group of four students. Optionally, design your own version of the game—see *Author's Note* below.

---

1 Divide the class into groups of four and give each group a die, a playing board, and the rules. Give each student a different playing piece. If no playing pieces are available, students can simply write their initials on small squares of paper or cardboard.

2 Tell the students to read the rules and start playing. Stay attentive but keep in the background. Only intervene when a group cannot decide if a sentence is correct or when they have made an incorrect decision. Try not to interrupt, but keep an ear open for points you might want to work on in later lessons.

3 When the game is over, go through the sentences, or at least ask if there are any sentences that the students are still questioning. If one group finishes a long time before the others, they may be asked to plan their own "Snakes and Ladders" playing board while the others finish.

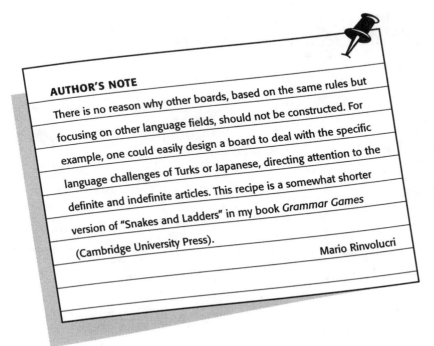

AUTHOR'S NOTE

There is no reason why other boards, based on the same rules but focusing on other language fields, should not be constructed. For example, one could easily design a board to deal with the specific language challenges of Turks or Japanese, directing attention to the definite and indefinite articles. This recipe is a somewhat shorter version of "Snakes and Ladders" in my book *Grammar Games* (Cambridge University Press).

Mario Rinvolucri

		Finish **70**	Do your friend want to stay? **69**	They came? **68**	Why didn't you was able to come? **67**
Which of them liked you best? **61**	**62**	How many does she wants? **63**	**64**	How about dropping around to see us? **65**	Who ate what? **66**
60	Which car liked you best? **59**	**58**	Who told him that? **57**	**56**	Why said he that? **55**
49	**50**	Must you really go? **51**	**52**	Did he wanted to see me? **53**	**54**
Why not tell them? **48**	**47**	Do you must tell her? **46**	**45**	What did you want? **44**	**43**
What does he think? **37**	**38**	What happened? **39**	**40**	They not like me? **41**	**42**
36	**35**	What want you? **34**	**33**	Can you come with me tonight? **32**	**31**
25	What you think? **26**	**27**	Who did you speak to? **28**	**29**	Who came? **30**
Why did she come? **24**	**23**	Was they with us? **22**	**21**	Spoke they at the meeting? **20**	**19**
Did he was here yesterday? **13**	**14**	**15**	Who spoke at the meeting? **16**	**17**	Did she spoke at the meeting? **18**
12	Was he here yesterday? **11**	**10**	He was here yesterday? **9**	**8**	**7**
Start **1**	Do you can come with me tonight? **2**	**3**	Do you like coffee? **4**	**5**	Do your parent like coffee? **6**

Grammatical Snakes and Ladders

Rules

1 Put your playing pieces on the START square.

2 Decide who is going to begin and in which order you are going to play.

3 If you are the first player, roll your die and move forward the number of squares indicated.

4 If you land on a sentence, say whether it is correct or not. If you think there is a mistake in the sentence, correct it immediately.

5 Your group must then decide if you are right or not. (Ask your teacher only if you are completely unable to arrive at a decision.) If your group agrees with you, move an extra three squares forward. If they disagree, move back three squares. (Your turn is now finished, so if you have landed on another sentence you may not give an opinion on its correctness.)

6 If you land on a blank square, you simply stay where you are until your next turn. If you land on a square where another person's playing piece is already standing, move forward one square. This rule applies whether you land on a sentence or on a blank square.

7 At your next turn, move your playing piece the number of squares shown on the die. For example, if you are on square 16 and the die shows five dots, move your playing piece to square 21.

8 Each player proceeds the same way, starting always at square 1 (START).

9 To finish, you must land directly on square 70. If you are on square 68 and throw a six, count two forward and four back to land on square 66 (and hope you throw a four on your next turn!).

75 **Throw a Conversation**

Level
High intermediate
and above

20

Language Function
Discussing a
predetermined subject

MATERIALS

One die per group
of seven students

BEFORE CLASS

Requires no preparation!

1 Write the following table on the board. Divide the class into groups of seven (if possible) and explain the game to them. Tell them that they are going to discuss a subject.

Throws of dice will determine how long the discussion will be, what the subject will be, what their attitude toward it will be, and how many students will take part.

Throw	Time in minutes	Subject	Personal attitude	Number
	1	parents	proud	7
	2	food	aggressive	6
	3	home	shy	5
	4	foreign languages	happy	4
	5	us	sad	3
	6	work	stern	2

2 Explain that one student throws the die. The number he or she throws determines the time in minutes the discussion will take. For example, ⚄ means five minutes. The next student throws to determine the subject; ⚂, for example, means home. The third student throws to determine the personal attitude of the students to the topic; for example, ⚀ means proud. The next student throws to determine the number of participants the conversation will have; for example, ⚅ means two. This student also chooses those to be involved. Using the above throws as an example, we see that two selected students have to speak for five minutes about home in a proud way.

3 While the selected students hold their conversation, the others should listen to make sure that they do not deviate from the subject. The language should also be checked and the listeners should note whether or not the mood is appropriate. One of the listeners should be appointed as a timekeeper. After each conversation the students who did not participate should be asked to comment on what they heard. About two or three rounds of the game should be enough for each lesson. Stay in the background as much as possible, but keep a close watch on what's going on.

Author
Christine Frank

Blind Man's Bluff

MATERIALS

Blindfolds

A large room where
students can move about

BEFORE CLASS

Requires no preparation!

Level
All

20

Language Function
Giving instructions

1 Teach or review with the class the following terms and concepts: *left, right, straight ahead, stop, turn around,* plus any other vocabulary you feel will be useful for the activity. This will, to a large extent, depend on the level of the class.

2 Move most of the furniture away from the center of the room but leave several objects such as chairs or small tables in the middle to serve as obstacles. Divide the class into pairs and tell the students to stand around the sides of the room, well away from the center. One partner in each pair is to put on a blindfold. The other plays the part of the guide.

3 The object of the game is to direct one's partner to the opposite side of the room without his or her touching any of the furniture or any of the other students. The guide gives directions using the vocabulary mentioned in Step 1. On reaching the other side, partners swap roles (and the blindfold). It is now the original guide's turn to be guided while the other partner gives the directions.

4 A scoring system can be used if you think the students would like one. Award one point to the guide every time the "blind person" disobeys an instruction and hits something, and one point to the "blind person" when the guide gives him or her a false instruction resulting in a collision.

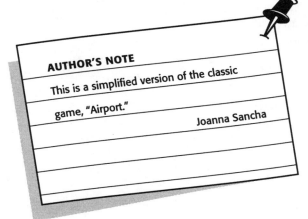

AUTHOR'S NOTE

This is a simplified version of the classic game, "Airport."

Joanna Sancha

Island Game

Level
Intermediate

30–50

Language Functions
Comparing and justifying decisions

Exchanging information

MATERIALS	BEFORE CLASS
Map (page 101)	Prepare copies of the map (one for each pair of students). Either use the example on the next page or draw your own island, provided it is on a similar numbered and lettered grid.

1 Brainstorm details that can be found on maps, such as rivers, resorts, industrial areas, roads, airports, nature reserves, tourist attractions, cities, and forests. Make a list on the board.

2 Divide the class into pairs and give each pair a copy of the map. Ask each pair to fill in their maps together, discussing where to put such features as have already been mentioned in Step 1. Students should use the map to build up the picture of a whole society. Encourage them to name the island and the cities, specify the natural resources, and so on. The more details they include, the more interesting the exercise becomes. Each pair may decide whether their map is large scale or small scale. Some may view it as an entire nation, other as just a speck in the sea. Circulate, correcting mistakes, asking students to explain what they have filled in and providing help with the language as necessary.

3 Give each pair another blank map. Then seat each pair opposite another, and ask the two pairs to exchange information about their respective islands. The information should be dictated and the blanks filled in with the details of the opposite pair's map but *without looking at it.* This is made possible by using the reference grid, for example: "A river flows from A2 to D3, passing through B2 and C3." "There's a small industrial park just south of the capital, which is in the middle of D2." Only when all the information has been taken down may the one pair see the other's map. Invite discussion and comparison of the attempted copies. If necessary, end the activity before all the details have been completed. Don't let the exchange go on so long that it becomes boring. Finish with a short general discussion.

Author
Randal Holme

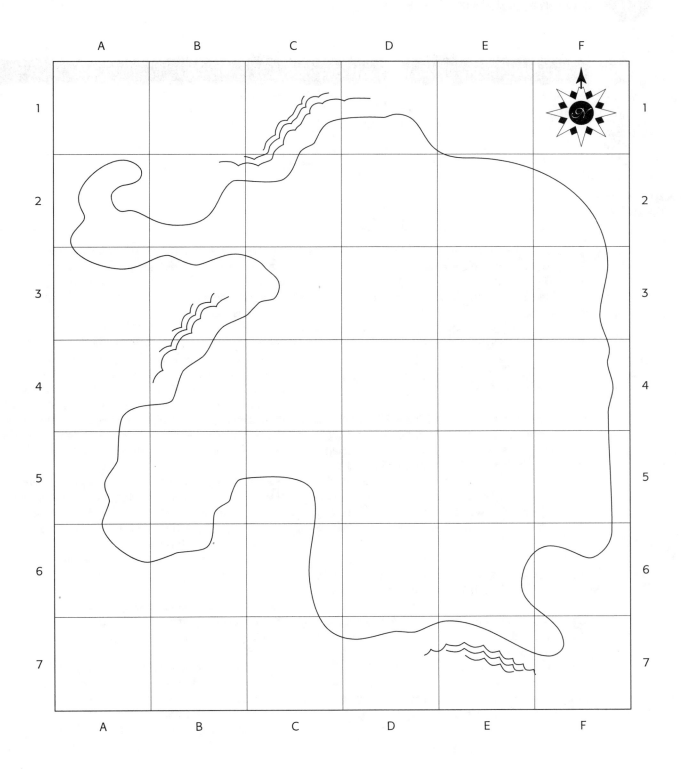

78 ✎ **Inverted Sentence Tree**

Level
Low intermediate
and above

15–
30

Language Function
Writing sentences

MATERIALS	BEFORE CLASS
None	Requires no preparation!

1 Tell the class they are going to make a sentence tree. Explain that because it is easier to read down than up, the tree will be inverted, that is turned upside down. (A sample tree is at the end of the recipe.) Put a diagram on the board like this:

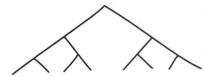

Tell the class that they will be adding words, putting out new branches after each word (until they have eight branches) to make sentences. The sentences should be as long as possible. Explain that the students will be working in teams, with members from each team taking turns at the board. Point out that team members will be penalized for adding words that cannot make a sentence, and add any other scoring rules you wish (see Step 7).

2 Divide the class into two teams, A and B. Each team will take turns sending members up to the board one by one. Each student should go to the board at least once.

3 Ask one of the members of Team A to start by writing a word that could be the beginning of a sentence on the board. This word should be written as high on the board as possible, in the center, and the writer should have at least two sentences in mind that could start with it. After the word has been written, the writer draws two "branches" down from it, like this:

4 Now have Team B send someone to the board to write a word for each branch and draw in two new branches under each word. Before sitting down, this person should read aloud the two partial sentences he or she has created.

5 Additions are now made by another member of Team A to create a total of eight branches. Further additions, by members of Teams A and B alternately, involve adding words to existing branches without creating new branches. Each member should add a word to each of the branches that is still incomplete. Each member should read aloud all the sentences or sentence fragments to which he or she has contributed.

6 Each group should check the other's performance and should challenge anything that is considered inappropriate. When challenged, a writer must give an acceptable sentence (or sentences) he or she has in mind when writing. This rule should be applied strictly to avoid non-sentences or sentences that are grammatically incorrect.

7 Keep score, or appoint a class member from each team to do so. With more advanced groups you may wish to give bonus points for the appropriate use of conjunctions or relative pronouns, thus rewarding the formation of complex sentences. You may also wish to take points off for each mistake, for being forced to "pass" (in which case the other group sends up its next member) or for finishing a sentence (thus rewarding the formation of longer sentences). The rules you set will depend on how competitive you want to make the task.

Inverted Sentence Tree continued... 78

Restrictions

A Note that you may have to limit the number of branches according to the level of your group. In any event it's suggested that you restrict them to an absolute number of eight or the exercise may get out of control. For advanced groups capable of producing very long sentences, an overhead projector with a rolling transparency would be ideal.

B If you wish, you can restrict the choice of first words, for example, to question words or auxiliaries where these need practice. You may also wish to specify that a particular word or structure be used.

Variations

A With smaller classes it may be better to make this a collective exercise, rather than dividing the class into teams. In this case, let the students call out their words to you, or better still, to a "secretary" who writes them on the board.

B Once the group is familiar with the rules, you can let them work in pairs. This can be made more competitive, if you wish, by rewarding the pair with the shortest, longest, or most complex sentence(s). Working in pairs may also be used to help individual students in a particular area of grammar, for example the use of auxiliaries in questions or negatives.

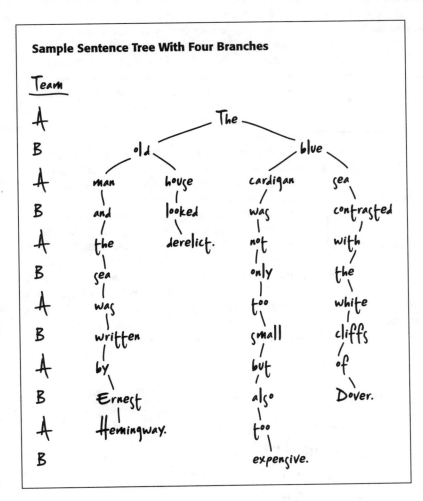

Sample Sentence Tree With Four Branches

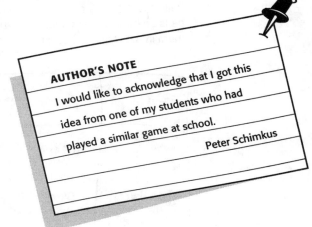

AUTHOR'S NOTE

I would like to acknowledge that I got this idea from one of my students who had played a similar game at school.

Peter Schimkus

79 Generating Expressions

Level
Low intermediate and above

⏱ 5–10

Language Function
Creating idiomatic expressions

MATERIALS

None

BEFORE CLASS

Select an expression such as "She's the apple of her father's eye" that has already been used in your class.

1 Draw three columns on the board. In the case of this expression the first column is for different sorts of fruits, the second for family members, and the third for parts of the body. Elicit items from the students and write them in the respective columns, for example:

Fruit	Family	Part of Body
pear	sister	stomach
strawberry	cousin	head
banana	uncle	elbow

Build up a collection of eight to ten words in each column. Let the students explain any new words to each other.

2 Coax the group into remembering the expression you selected before class and write it above the word lists. Ask the group why the expression should be specifically "the apple of one's father's eye." Are there no other possibilities that are equally descriptive? What about some combinations from the three lists you have collected? Ask the students to read across (or diagonally across) the columns to form new possibilities such as "She's the apricot of her nephew's knee."

Variation

A variation for lower levels is to base the activity on typical British pub names. (With students unfamiliar with such names, you should write several on the board, either real or fictitious.) "The Bishop's Finger," for example, would generate suggestions based on a combination of professions and parts of the body, say: "The Nurse's Ankle" or "The Engineer's Eye." (Higher levels could do these exercises as a lead-in to more serious work, perhaps a project on the origin of English and American sayings and "folk" names for places or objects.) Of course most of the variations generated are ridiculous, but then so are the originals—unless you find out where they came from.

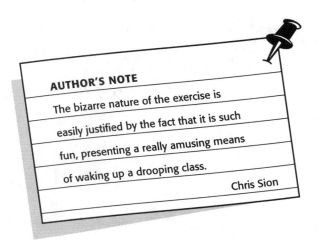

AUTHOR'S NOTE

The bizarre nature of the exercise is easily justified by the fact that it is such fun, presenting a really amusing means of waking up a drooping class.

Chris Sion

Riddle Scramble

MATERIALS

Small cards
(approximately postcard size)

Riddles (page 106)

BEFORE CLASS

Select some riddles appropriate to the level of your class. It is important that the students understand the vocabulary or the humor will be lost on them. For classes of up to ten or twelve students pick out one riddle per person. For larger classes it is probably better to have two or three sets of riddles, for example two sets of eight for a class of sixteen. You can find some examples on page 106. Note that two of these depend on homonyms, words that sound the same but have different meanings and, in this case, spellings.

Draw horizontal lines on each card to divide it into four equal sections. The four sections correspond to the question and answer parts of two riddles. Label them Q, A, Q, A. Write the question part of one riddle in the top Q section, and the answer part of another riddle in the bottom A section of each card, as shown in the example at the end of this activity. Arrange the material so that the missing part of each riddle is to be found on another card. Make sure that the riddles are split up so that each student has to ask *two* others in order to complete his or her card. This requires a clear mind and a little organization, but is not at all as complicated as it may sound!

Level

Low intermediate
and above

Language Function

Analyzing and combining
questions and answers

1 Explain the activity to the class. Tell them they must find the missing questions and answers. (I do not usually tell them they are working with riddles, which are supposed to be funny. I just wait for the light to dawn.) Make sure the students understand that they have *two separate* questions and answers. Encourage them to say the questions and answers out loud. They should not simply show their cards to each other.

2 Give each student a card. Tell them to wander about, asking questions and trying out their answers until they make the proper connections. They should fill in the cards when they have found the correct question or

answer. Provide help with vocabulary as required, but stay in the background as much as possible so that students may work things out for themselves.

3 Get students to ask their riddles of others who do not know the answers. A further, optional activity is to tell the class to put their cards away and reconstruct the riddles from memory. You will need to circulate to make sure the riddles are correct.

Author

Heidi Yorkshire

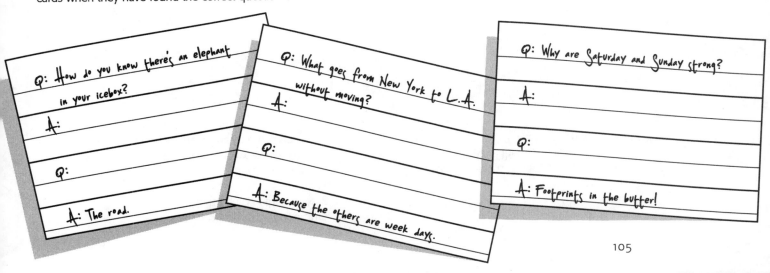

Riddles
Answers are listed below, upside down.

1. What can you have after someone has taken it?

2. Why do birds fly south for the winter?

3. What goes from New York to L.A. without moving?

4. What's white outside, green inside, and jumps?

5. Why are Saturday and Sunday strong?

6. Why is an empty pocketbook always the same?

7. Where does Friday come before Thursday?

8. What can you hold without touching it?

9. What gets bigger the more you take away from it?

10. Why did Bill take a tape measurer to bed?

11. What animal can jump higher than a house?

12. How do you know there's an elephant in your refrigerator?

1. Your picture.
2. It's quicker than walking.
3. The road.
4. A frog sandwich.
5. Because the others are week (weak) days.
6. Because there's never any change in it.
7. In the dictionary.
8. Your breath.
9. A hole.
10. He wanted to see how long he slept.
11. All of them. A house can't jump.
12. Footprints in the butter!

You Had a Dream

Level
Low intermediate
and above

15–30

Language Function
Asking questions

MATERIALS	BEFORE CLASS
None	Requires no preparation!

1 Select two talkative students (see *Author's Note,* #1) and tell them to come out of the room with you to prepare an activity. Ask the others to remain quietly in class. This stage should only take a couple of minutes.

2 Tell the two students to imagine that they have had a dream that they cannot remember (see *Author's Note,* #2). Strange as it may seem, they both had the identical dream. Make it clear that this is only a game and not some sort of sinister psychological test. Explain that the rest of the students *do* know the contents of the dream and will help the two remember it. Tell them to prepare questions about the dream to establish what happened. However, the rest of the class may only answer "Yes" or "No." Questions such as "Where did it happen?" are not acceptable and need to be replaced by "Did it happen in the United States?", "Was it in New York City?", and so on. Leave the two to prepare as many questions as they can and return to the classroom.

3 Tell the rest of the class what you have told the two selected students and explain how to respond to the questions, namely: Questions ending with the letters AEIOU or Y are answered "Yes," and those ending with consonants "No." The manner in which the dream develops depends entirely on the questions.

For example:
Was it a nightmar**e**? (Yes)
Was it a bad drea**m**? (No)
Did I see a member of my famil**y**? (Yes)
Did I know the perso**n**? (No)
Was the girl prett**y**? (Yes)
Was the girl beautifu**l**? (No)

It is vitally important that this system is understood before the questions begin.

4 Call the two "dreamers" back into the room and tell them to ask their questions. The bizarre answers are easily explained by pointing out that it is only a dream. Dreams do not follow the logic of everyday life. Should the activity not get off the ground, or should the questioners lose inspiration, you may want to prompt them by saying, for instance: "Why not ask what you were wearing?" or "You could try asking about where you were and who else was there." If the questioners do not manage to "crack the code" draw the game to a close before it goes on too long.

5 Follow up the activity by asking the "dreamers" what they felt, what they found particularly confusing, why they repeated questions over and over, and so on. If the group is interested you might continue with a discussion centered on recent dreams, recurring dreams, the psychology of dreams, and related topics.

AUTHOR'S NOTE

1 It is also possible to do this activity with three or even four students asking the questions. However, it is not advisable to select only one student as it tends to isolate him or her from the class and creates too much pressure to think of questions.

2 This activity can be turned into a more specific exercise by focusing it on something relevant to your class, say: You had a dream about a bank/your job/a hospital/a new engineering project.

3 I would like to acknowledge that I originally got this idea from Susan Davies.

Chris Sion

Index

Instant Recipes
(activities that require no preparation)

Recipes by Level

Recipes by Language Function

Colophon

Text set in Formata Light and Medium, with margin
notes set in Formata Condensed Light and Medium;
© 1991 Adobe Systems Incorporated, trademark of
H. Berthold AG. Titles set in Spumoni LP; © 1997 Adobe
Systems Incorporated, trademark of LetterPerfect Design.
Table of Contents level icons set in Memphis Extra Bold;
© 1988 Adobe Systems Incorporated, trademark of the
Linotype Company.

Featuring a special appearance of the handwritten
typefaces Splurge Regular and Bold, designed by
Amy Conger; © 1994–2001 l'Abécédarienne.